A KINGDOM WE CAN TASTE

A KINGDOM WE CAN TASTE

Sermons for the Church Year

David A. Davis

William B. Eerdmans Publishing Company

Grand Rapids, Michigan / Cambridge, U.K.

Published 2007 by

Wm. B. Eerdmans Publishing Co.

2140 Oak Industrial Drive N.E., Grand Rapids, Michigan 49505 /

P.O. Box 163, Cambridge CB3 9PU U.K.

www.eerdmans.com

Printed in the United States of America

12 11 10 09 08 07   7 6 5 4 3 2 1

Library of Congress Cataloging-in-Publication Data

Davis, David A.

A kingdom we can taste: sermons for the church year /

David A. Davis.

p.   cm.

ISBN 0-8028-2747-0 (pbk.: alk. paper)

1. Church year sermons. 2. Presbyterian Church — Sermons.

I. Title.

BV30.D37   2007

252′.6 — dc22

2007026263

Contents

⌒⅏⌒

v

Contents

Contents

Introduction

Advent and Lent come around every year. So do Easter and Christmas. The rhythm of the liturgical year conveys God's promise. However, for the pastor, the steady movement of the calendar brings the challenge of preaching the occasions and seasons year after year. Most preachers know the anxiety that comes when trying to find something new to say. Those who listen to sermons must feel something of the repetition when the feast-day sermons come around. This collection arises out of my belief that both preachers and hearers of the Word participate in the preaching moment. Both can enrich the experience and contribute to the newness of the gospel proclaimed.

These sermons arise out of the preaching life at Nassau Presbyterian Church in Princeton, New Jersey, where I have served as pastor for seven years. My own experience of a shared preaching life also reaches back to fourteen years of ministry at the First Presbyterian Church of Blackwood, New Jersey. I have been blessed as a pastor to serve two congregations where corporate worship and the event of proclamation have been the joyful center of life together.

Introduction

The hearers of the Word in these communities of faith have taught me so much about preaching. They have helped me to understand the promise of the gospel and to give witness to the presence of God in the ordinary places of life. They have been willing to listen to and participate in an ongoing conversation about biblical texts, discipleship, and life as a community of faith. No sermon is ever the first word or the last word. Faithful preaching takes place within the ebb and flow of the church's life, within the web of pastoral realities and concerns, within the cycles of people's lives. My preaching grows out of the rich context of the church's life together.

So I lift these sermons out of their congregational context as examples of this communal sharing. Meaning in a sermon is ultimately a shared construction. The fullness of the parish context gives a sermon life, not simply because preaching is an oral event, but because preaching depends upon the church. Dietrich Bonhoeffer once said in a lecture on homiletics that "I preach, because the church is there — and I preach, that the church might be there. Church preaches to church."[1]

This sermon collection comes with my conviction that preaching belongs to the church. Though one person rises to speak, it is a corporate act of proclamation. In the power of the Holy Spirit, the Word of God is experienced not at the lips of the preacher, nor simply in the ears of one listener, but in the shared experience of the gospel proclaimed amid the church's collective act of praise.

---

1. Dietrich Bonhoeffer, *Worldly Preaching: Lectures on Homiletics,* edited and translated by Clyde E. Fant (New York: Crossroad, 1991), p. 112.

A Kingdom We Can Taste

Walking Still

ISAIAH 2:2-5

The Word of the Lord. An oracle of Isaiah. In days to come. In prophet's voice. In days to come. "In days to come the mountain of the LORD's house shall be established as the highest of the mountains, and shall be raised above the hills; all the nations shall stream to it." A word of the Lord that emanates from deep within the history of God's people. In days to come. "Many peoples shall come and say, 'Come, let us go up to the mountain of the LORD, to the house of the God of Jacob.'" That the Lord may teach. That we may walk in the Lord's paths. In days to come. A prophetic voice that echoes, that repeats, that never fades.

In days to come. It comes not just from Isaiah but from Micah too. You remember the question that made Micah famous: "What does the LORD require of you but to do justice, and to love kindness, and to walk humbly with your God?" In days to come. Micah proclaimed it as well. In prophets' voice. That's now plural. In days to come. That teaching shall go forth from Zion and the Word of the Lord from Jerusalem. It's not a piercing prophetic refrain, not a glorious trumpet sound, but more of a guttural groan.

In days to come. "[The LORD] shall judge between the nations, and shall arbitrate for many peoples; they shall beat their swords into plowshares, and their spears into pruning hooks."

Isaiah's oracle. Constant. Rhythmic. Played into every period of history. Bass notes plucked forever over there in the prophets' section of the orchestra. In days to come. In days to come. In days to come. "Nation shall not lift up sword against nation, neither shall they learn war any more." I guess we're not there yet. So play on, Isaiah. We're not there yet. We're still walking. We're walking still. So play on.

Wreath. Candle. Purple. Calendars sent home. "Come, Thou Long-Expected Jesus." "O Come, O Come, Emmanuel." It must be Advent, the beginning of the church's holiday season. Advent is happy new year. It is the beginning of a new year in terms of the church's liturgical calendar. We begin in terms of the life cycle of Jesus and the gestation in Mary's belly and the birth of a baby. Advent is John the Baptist. Advent is preparing the way. Imagine sermon after sermon in pulpit after pulpit in the weeks to come. Sermons about the difference between preparing and just waiting. Preachers all have a file full! Preparing for the coming of the Christ Child again and again and again. That's Advent.

And Advent is living that in-between, that gray area between the already and the not-yet. Indeed, the Lord has come, and we want at least to appear as though we are eager and ready and willing for Christ to come again! Advent is the end of Thanksgiving and the beginning of Christmas. Those weeks when anticipation builds, and the room gradually fills with color, and the children start to beam, and some of us demand Christmas carols while others of us hold out for some good Advent singing still this side of Bethlehem! "Rejoice! Rejoice! Emmanuel shall come to thee...." It must be Advent. Click on any of the above for your Advent theme of the day, or the week, or the season. Four candles. Four weeks. Advent. A kind of comfort food for the regular worshiper for whom church feels like home.

Just the other day, a church member introduced me to someone who has lived in this town a long time. He retired when I was
about ten. I think he mentioned that he was eighty-five, though I
would never have guessed. Our conversation was light fare, like
the lunch we shared. It was only later, when he and I had a moment to ourselves, when just the two of us found ourselves away
from the others, it was only then that he followed up on the introduction that had identified me as pastor of Nassau Presbyterian
Church. "So what do you say to people who worry about the state
of the world?" I hesitated, trying to wrap my head around the sud-
den shift from just talking about the weather. He went on: "Thou-
sands of years, and we're still fighting each other and killing each
other. It makes no sense — all the death and destruction. It's not
getting any better. How can there be a God?" Wishing we were still
talking about the good old days around town, I tried a bit of Cal-
vinism. "I'm not sure God is the one to blame here. Don't you think
it's more humanity's utter failure, humankind's total depravity?"
My effort was a bit weak, and he got a bit defensive. "I'm not de-
praved," he said with some bristle. And then, after thinking some
more, he commented, "Well, it's not my problem. I'm not going to
be around much more. What about your generation, or the next?"

What about the days to come? That's what he was asking. It
was only later that I decided his question was less intellectual,
less theological. It wasn't about theodicy or philosophy. I don't
think he was looking for debate, or was expecting some magic answer from me. In hindsight, I think it was an opportunity for pastoral care, an opportunity that I mostly missed. This stranger no
longer, I think he just wanted some care and companionship in
his angst. He was looking for some comfort when reading the
morning newspaper. He was yearning for some assurance when
looking out at the world. His only expectation was a little bit of
hope for his grandchildren. Without wading into politics or foreign policy at all, he was shrugging his shoulders and throwing up
his arms: "How about a little peace?" In days to come.

I think he was asking me about Advent. No, he certainly wasn't inquiring about the calendar or the babe in a manger. He wasn't wanting to talk about "Prepare ye the way of the Lord" or "the delay of the parousia" (that second coming of Christ). This was no shallow conversation about the holiday! But he was asking me about Advent, about the days to come. In days to come. In days to come. Swords into plowshares. Spears into pruning hooks. Learning war no more. In days to come. That's Advent. Because there's this prophet's voice that just won't quit!

We must still be walking, because we're clearly not there yet. Those prophets' voice, the prophets' plural voice, the prophet's oracle includes an appeal, a reminder, an affirmation for those of us who find ourselves no longer strangers along this worn pathway of life and faith. A word to those of us yet trying to make some sense of what we see, trying to name some purpose. A word to those of us who pray with more than a hint of urgency, "Is a little more peace out of the question?" In days to come? What about now? And the Word of the Lord plays on. "But we will walk in the name of the LORD our God forever and ever!" That's Micah. Isaiah is just as clear. "O house of Jacob, come, let us walk in the light of the LORD!" Yes, we're walking still. It must be Advent.

A long time ago I organized a weekend work trip to my family's cabin in the Endless Mountains of Pennsylvania. The plan for this "men's retreat" called for the interior to be finished with tongue-and-groove cedar. Not being particularly sure of my ability to complete such a task, nor being too proud to ask for help, I had invited about five or six guys who had the necessary skills. Late one night, as we all were safely snuggled into sleeping bags after a long day's work, the lights were off, and the darkness of the woods settled all around inside the cabin. After a period of silence, which was clearly long enough for some important thoughts and bedtime prayers, one of the men made the following observation. "You're not going to believe this," he said, as if sharing a new discovery, "but it's darker with my eyes open than it is with my eyes shut!"

Wreath. Candle. Purple. New year. Weeks to go before Christmas. Prepare ye the way. Yes, of course. But when it is darker when your eyes are open, when it is so uncomfortably, frighteningly, overwhelmingly dark, when the reality of the world simply magnifies the darkness that comes in broken relationships. Sometimes darkness comes in a conversation with a doctor about a diagnosis, or in the deaf ear offered by your parents, or in the worry for one of your children, or in the caring for a dying parent, or in stress at work, or in the urgency that comes with no work, or in the terrifying prospects of college admission, or in the unrelenting power of depression, or in the exhaustion that comes long before the end of the week, or in the helpless feeling of losing your independence, or in the overwhelming sense that everyone in your sixth-period class hates you. Darkness comes. For when any sense that there is a God seems laughable, when the notion of resurrection and life eternal has long since been lost on you, when it seems darker when your eyes are wide open — even then the prophets' voice, it just won't quit. In days to come. In days to come.

And together, you and I, we will be walking still, walking in the light of the Lord. Finding comfort in God's grace. Hearing assurance by God's mercy. Sensing hope in God's promise. While basking in God's presence, still crying out for more peace. That's Advent.

We shall walk God's paths together. Teaching shall go forth from Zion and Jerusalem. Teaching about plowshares, pruning hooks, learning war no more.... Come, even if for just a taste! The table is set for days to come.

The Absurdity of Our Preparation

MATTHEW 3:1-12

One morning a postcard arrived in the church office that stopped me in my tracks. A family in the church had sent the card during their trip to Glacier National Park in Montana. "Imagine our surprise," the card said, "when we saw a picture here in Many Glacier Hotel, a picture of Rev. Davis standing with the other bellmen, complete with lederhosen, kneesocks, and bow tie." To my knowledge, the picture itself hasn't made its way back to Princeton. That summer of 1984 I was working as a park chaplain with a Christian ministry in the national park. My day job, however, was that of a bellman in the century-old, chalet-type hotel. It was the Swiss theme that carried over into the uniform for the bellmen (not the bellboys).

As I look back, one of the more striking responsibilities of the bell staff required us to be the initial response team in the case of any fire in that all-wooden building in the middle of a national park. Over and over again we practiced and prepared for our fire response. A typical drill never changed. The fire alarm went off. The bellmen ran to the front desk. There we were told the location of the alarm. We were given hard hats and gloves. On the way to the location we picked up a few fire extinguishers. Got to the room. Felt the door for heat. Opened the door with the master key. And there, staring back at us, would be one of the maintenance men, standing on a chair holding a burning candle under a detector. He looked at his watch, wrote down the response time, then looked at us — a half-dozen young men in leather shorts, kneesocks, white shirts, and bow ties, wearing hard hats and gloves and carrying fire extinguishers. And the maintenance man couldn't stop laughing.

Our preparations were never tested for real that summer. One would have to wonder about the efficiency and the effectiveness of our rather feeble response team. Of course we went over the drill again and again. But in reality there was a touch of absurdity to it all. We were bellmen hired to carry luggage, hoping and praying that nothing more serious would happen.

I wonder what the Child Jesus must think about the absurdity of our preparation this time of year. Advent leads to Christmas year after year. We go over it and over it. You know the yearly routines and rituals during these weeks of preparation. For most of us they change little, and most of them happen beyond these walls. The Christ Child rests there on the straw and looks out as we rush to the scene, bumbling, falling over one another, exhausted from the Advent practice and the Christmas preparation. This year our rather feeble "Adventian" community will fall once again at Bethlehem's door, trying to straighten our hats and attempting frantically to dust off the distractions. With a cleansing breath on Christmas Eve, we will try to attend to the birth of a Savior. I wonder what the Christ Child must think.

There's an absurdity to our preparation. And yet, year after year we dare to hope that something more serious will happen. We dare to believe the kingdom of God is in our midst. We look around at this unimpressive, collective response team, and we dare to believe that we are the church. Even in those years when the violence, the devastation, the suffering in the world doesn't just trickle but flows like a river. Even in those years when all of us struggle to find a new worldview that will help us wrestle with unanswered questions and process words like "terror" and "evil." Even in years like that, in years like this, even then we will fall to our knees before the manger and dare to tell ourselves once again that God is with us.

Smack in the midst of all the absurdity of Advent, the voice of John the Baptist comes bellowing down the hall. Like the rather eccentric uncle who embarrasses you at the family picnic, he begins broadcasting, his voice cutting through the small talk and the mindless chatter and the yearly routines of life. With its own brand of timeless absurdity, the Baptist's cry once again shatters the noise of these days of preparation. With a camel-hair coat, a leather belt, and a plate full of locusts, it is John and that prophetic voice. It is John and his witness to the Messiah. "Repent, for the kingdom of heaven has come near." "Prepare the way of the Lord." "Bear fruit worthy of repentance." It is John's voice that somehow assures us once again that despite the absurdity of our Advent preparation, we shall still encounter the One who baptizes with the Holy Spirit and with fire. Because in Matthew's Gospel, John came preaching "in those days": "In those days John the Baptist appeared in the wilderness of Judea."

In the Gospel of Mark, John the Baptist is something like the fancy capital letter at the beginning of a chapter in a rare book. Mark begins with the Baptist. In Luke's Gospel, a narrative of the birth of John the Baptist serves as something of an overture, an introduction to God's plan and to angels and to speechless parents. John — well, the Gospel of John sets up the Baptist as something of a philosophical instrument, a directional tool. "There was a man sent from God, whose name was John. He came as a witness to testify to the light, so that all might believe through him. He himself was not the light, but he came to testify to the light" (1:6-8).

But Matthew's John the Baptist comes to the stage "in those days." "In those days John the Baptist appeared in the wilderness of Judea, proclaiming, 'Repent, for the kingdom of heaven has come near.'" Most would assume that Matthew is simply referring to the early days of the public ministry of Jesus: "in those days." Some would point to a more cosmic sense: the first days of the new kingdom era ushered in by the Messiah, the Son of God, born from Mary's womb — "in THOSE days." But in the first few chapters of Matthew, John arrives long after the birth of Jesus. John's voice is heard after the Wise Men have come from the East. Mary and Joseph have already taken the child with them in their flight to Egypt. Infuriated, King Herod slaughters the young children in and around Bethlehem, and Matthew writes of the voice in Ramah and tells of Rachel weeping. Only after Herod's death and some vivid dreams does the family return to settle in Nazareth.

All of that happens before John the Baptist appears on the scene. If you follow the plot of Matthew's story, it is "in those days" that John comes to preach about preparation, repentance, bearing fruit, and the dangers of presumption, birthright, and family coattails when it comes to faith. In those days when the birth of Jesus seems less about heavenly choirs rejoicing and more about God's promise, God's faithfulness, and God's fulfillment. In those days when the wise and worldly search for meaning and the powerful are threatened by the hope of a messianic kingdom where the hungry are fed, the poor are lifted up, and the oppressed are set free. In those days when the journeys of life take the faithful to places unknown and the lament is of biblical proportions, when the earthly songs of heartache seem louder than the heavenly songs of praise, when fear, warnings, and disconcerting dreams motivate the people of God and the divine angels with those fluttering words "Do not be afraid" are just a little harder to find. "In those days" comes John the Baptist. In those days. In these days.

One of my teachers in speech and preaching told me of a Christmas Eve years ago when he was a pastor serving a congre-

gation. He had become overly frustrated with all the shallow cere-
mony of Christmas, the "Hallmark cardness" of it all. So he rose to
preach on Matthew's Christmas. He took on that "slaughter of the
innocents": Herod's destruction of life. It is far from the harmoni-
ous scene of a creation at peace, a silent night, and a little child
leading them. The story told by Matthew has a truthful edge, a
certain "other side," a certain harshness, a certain gut-wrenching
light that illumines the darkness of the world. The professor told
me of the look on people's faces as they left church that night.
They were a bit speechless at the door, not knowing what to say to
him after he preached a sermon on Christmas Eve about Herod
killing children, after he preached a sermon about "those days."

But there is a truthfulness to "those days." And there is an
honesty of faith and a truthfulness to these days, in an Advent
season when the brokenness of the world is so apparent and
those close to you know such suffering, in an Advent season when
the darkness around us forces the light of the Christ Child to
shine even brighter. And there is a certain absurdity to all our
preparation. In the midst of it all, John the Baptist stands up,
bearing with him the weight of a prophetic voice, and calls out
"Repent!" John sees those Pharisees and Sadducees coming, lead-
ers of faith divided by so much opinion. John looks at such a people, a people defined by what divides them, and he pleads for life,
asks for a fruit of faith that would bear witness to the Spirit of
God. John dares to stand among the people of God rushing to the
Nativity, and he reminds them that they can't just inherit the
name "church."

John stands in the midst of those days, and he stands in the
midst of these days. He looks around at the absurdity of our preparation and points to the One who will baptize with the Holy
Spirit and with fire. He takes center stage only to point to the Messiah. His voice booms among us to call us to encounter the Savior,
who is Christ the Lord. The One who is more powerful than John.
The One who is coming. Indeed, we are not worthy to carry his

sandals, but he empowers us to be his people. By his love we know ourselves to be his friends. By God's grace we are molded into his body for the world. By that same Spirit, you and I bear witness to his light. The world seems darker, but surely the light of Christ is here among us.

Like you, I have listened to John the Baptist break through the shallow realities of Advent for years. That word of judgment comes to shake and threaten everything from Advent calendars that give chocolate to our most calloused and overdone rituals of family and faith. Prepare. Repent. Bear fruit. You and I have heard that voice before, that voice of judgment.

But this year, this Advent, I have to tell you, that voice sounds more like a promise.

Traveling Mercies

ISAIAH 35:1-10

It is a liturgical tradition as sacred as any other. It is that Sunday in Advent reserved for special music. Just a few weeks before Christmas, and the Sabbath morning includes a collection of carols or an oratorio or a cantata. Pinkham's *Christmas Cantata* plays well that Sunday. The movement is simple: from shepherds telling the story to *magnum mysterium* to "Glory to God in the highest," from majestic to slow to fast. A strikingly brief Christmas cantata heard from start to finish. One evening I dropped by choir rehearsal to listen. I found myself wondering what notes ought to linger in your ear when you listen to this piece of music. An easy answer would be those last "Alleluias" intended for full voice, with the sopranos soaring and the organ and the trumpets and the full choir coming to such triumphant resolution.

But here's another focus to consider, another climax, an exclamation point that doesn't come at the end and doesn't come in double or triple forte! It is there in the very center of Pinkham's piece. There at the end of the second movement. The notes come from just the choir. They are sung with almost piercing quiet —

14

mysterious, wondrous, still. *Christum.* The word is *Christum.* "Our Christ." Between the majestic and the fast-paced, with "Alleluias" on both sides, as the brass falls silent, in an almost haunting way, the choir breathes the incarnation. *Dominum Christum.*

Actually, Pinkham's work loses something if sung only in English. In the Latin, Pinkham uses *Christum* only at this point in the cantata. In the first movement, the English translation has the choir singing "Born for us was Christ Jesus." However, in Latin they simply sing *"natum vidimus"*: "born for us, born for us, born, born, born for us." The singing of *Christum* is delayed. The title waits for the end of the second movement. The word comes in a whisper, there in the middle. For Pinkham, in the text as well as in the music, it is "Christ the center" (to quote a Bonhoeffer title).

You're not always supposed to hear from start to finish. A song. A poem. A text. From start to finish. That's not always "how a poem means" (to quote John Ciardi). Take Chapter 35 of Isaiah, for instance. Our Old Testament lesson for the third Sunday of Advent. The word of the prophet. The 35th chapter seems to stand alone, an oracle in and of itself, a poem to read about the blooming desert and the promise of God and a highway to travel and the return to Zion. But as with Pinkham's Christmas cantata, maybe you're not supposed to settle for reading it in one direction. One Old Testament scholar even suggests reading Isaiah 35 from the center, explaining which notes from this prophet's song ought to linger in your ear.

Between the desert blooming and the promise of everlasting joy, when "sorrow and sighing shall flee away," between "they shall see the glory of the LORD, the majesty of our God" and "the redeemed shall walk there, and the ransomed of the LORD shall return," between the weak hands and feeble knees being strengthened and the eyes of the blind being opened and the lame leaping and the speechless singing, between the picture of creation's miraculous transformation and the scene of the heavenly highway intended to be trumpeted in full voice, no doubt with soprano descant, between all of that the prophet whispers these words: "Here is your God."

God will come. God will come with power determined to avenge life and conquer death. God will come with a bounty of gifts sure to ripen as the harvest falls in the fullness of time. "Here is your God." The prophet speaks — a word, a promise so wondrous, so mysterious that all other words are drawn in, both sides of the poem turn to face the center. "Here is your God. . . . He will come and save you." *Dominum Christum.*

Isaiah 35. God's highway. Joy and gladness. No more sorrow. No more sighing. And if you're hearing only in one direction, if the church is reading from start to finish, you might not get it. But if you're willing to stand with both feet firmly planted and look far off to the divine horizon, then it would seem rather clear that this vision of Isaiah, the beauty of the Way, this Holy Way, must be heaven's highway. Where the glory of the Lord shall be revealed. Where all flesh shall see it together. Where they shall sing for ever and ever. Alleluia. Alleluia. Isaiah paints a picture of heaven. The highway of the saints starts at the gates of heaven, and the traveling mercies begin there on the other side, just inside the Pearly Gates.

Of course, you and I have to buckle our seat belts now, don't we? This faith of ours — it is a traveling faith. You see the same world I see. I watch the same news you watch. We share the same prayer list. There are no new doubts to invent; we have them all covered. There is both joy and concern in the hearts of God's people. There are those who feel themselves held tight by God, and those who would tell you that they are wandering beyond the edge of grace. Call it a roller coaster. Call it the ups and downs. Call it seeing the good with the bad. Or call it life in the community of faith. Call it a faith journey. Call it traveling on the Holy Way. Maybe the highway in heaven begins on the other side of glory, but you and I know that we are bumping and plodding and running and wandering and scratching and parading and falling and marching and living and dying and rising every single day. Because that's what faith is. We're traveling this highway together. And I for one can't settle for simply standing with both feet planted and keeping a stiff upper lip and squinting from here to eternity.

Just about when I'm ready to conclude that old Isaiah was just talking about heaven, just when I'm ready to proclaim this vision of the Holy Way as eternal rest in the everlasting arms of God, just about then Advent stares me right in the face. Just when I'm ready yet again to just hear in one direction, to read from front to back, from beginning to end, thinking all this heavenly faith does little earthly good, just when the faithful are ready to announce the kingdom of God as something we have to yet wait for, just about then the prophet suggests we sing this song from the center. This Good News poem, this mysterious promise of God, this gospel word, in the prophet's voice. Amid all the noise of this culture beyond moderation, amid the confusion of a world long suffering and far short on peace, amid the pace of life long since run out of control, the prophet whispers, "Here is your God." The prophet whispers. The choir breathes incarnation. *Dominum Christum.* Christ our Savior.

Advent means we start at the center. Christ the Center. Advent reminds us that the journey is now. We're on the highway. And God is with us. Christ is for us. Maybe I haven't seen the desert bloom, but I know some of you have. I must confess that I haven't seen blind eyes opened or deaf ears unstopped. And frankly, this road we travel is full of lions and other threats to faith and life. But when you read from the center, there is an already and a not-yet to the kingdom of God. There is a now and a then to faith. Because I have seen weak hands made strong. I have seen feeble knees made firm. I have seen you find the strength to live one more day by God's grace. I have watched you stare down the fear in your heart as you reached down deep and leaned again on the Rock of our Salvation. I have watched as you have discovered the very face of God in children on another continent who live in dire poverty, and as you have determined that the glory of God is to be seen in packing those groceries and stocking those shelves and serving up lunch at the soup kitchen.

I have walked along this kingdom way with you as you found out that the faith you affirm in confirmation at fourteen can give you strength when you are nineteen and away at college. When you had to learn that the abundant life you knew in forty-five years of life with your spouse would sustain you in the years of life alone. As you realized once again that the joy you've tasted by God's grace ought to be lived out in a commitment to God's justice. As you came to know that just a glimpse of the majesty of God can give you the strong hands and the firm knees to speak for those this culture would rather silence, and to serve those the economy would rather leave behind, and to give in a way that shatters the idolatry of selfishness. I have waded into the baptismal waters with you, celebrating the steadfast and unmerited love of God, utterly convinced that the kingdom was here in our midst. I have gathered with you at the grave as together we have proclaimed through tears, "'I am the resurrection and the life,' says the Lord. 'Those who believe in me, even though they die, yet shall they live!'"

It's a highway we're on. And we're marching to Zion. Singing with joy, maybe not from front to back, but from the center. Clinging to the traveling mercies God provides. That's Advent. God's whisper never to be drowned out by the world's shout. A whisper that breathes incarnation. God is here. God will save you. *Dominum Christum.*

Signs from a Weary God

ISAIAH 7:10-17

cwc

Prior to the sermon during this service of worship, we gathered at the baptismal font to celebrate the sacrament.

"Look, the young woman is with child and shall bear a son, and shall name him Emmanuel." Emmanuel means "God with us." In the first chapter of Matthew we read that the angel of the Lord appeared to Joseph in a dream and told him not to be afraid. "Take Mary as your wife. The child conceived in her is from the Holy Spirit." The angel said that she would have a son. Joseph was to name him "Jesus, for he will save his people from their sins." Then the Gospel writer, knowing full well that his audience would be attuned to the writings of the prophets, that any talk of the Messiah would have to be rooted in the lineage of David, lifts the quote from Isaiah: "Look, the virgin shall conceive and bear a son, and they shall name him Emmanuel."

So you never hear much about Ahaz, and Ephraim, and Judah, and the Syro-Ephraimite War, and King Tiglath-pileser of Assyria and the 700's B.C.E. You certainly don't hear much at Christmas when we're singing and lighting candles and waiting again for the Christ Child, God with us. You don't hear much about all of that from Matthew, or from other Advent preachers like me. You don't hear much of the biblical context in Advent.

Ahaz was the king of Judah. Judah was being threatened as the nations conspired and negotiated and maneuvered and fought for power. Specifically, the smaller countries of Israel and Syria were looking to overthrow Ahaz so that they could build a coalition (Israel/Syria/Judah) against the most powerful Assyria. However, Ahaz proved just as willing to align with the Assyrian empire, even paying for protection.

Amid such brutal, real, and apparently timeless nastiness among the nations, Isaiah spoke to Ahaz. Isaiah spoke as the heart of Ahaz and the heart of his people were afraid. Indeed, according to the sacred page, their hearts "shook as the trees of the forest shake before the wind" (Isa. 7:2).

Isaiah spoke into that context of great fear and tumult. "Ask for a sign, Ahaz. Ask for a sign that could plunge the very depths of hell. A sign that could soar to the highest heaven. Ask the Lord for a sign." The reply of Ahaz must have included some body language. "I will not. I will not ask. I will not put the Lord to the test. I will not." But Isaiah was not convinced by the king's attempt at piety. Maybe Isaiah was remembering the burning bush with Moses, or the bloody Nile, or the water from the rock, or the manna from heaven. Maybe Isaiah was remembering Gideon's fleece, or Elijah and that still, small voice at Mount Horeb. Maybe Isaiah was remembering the other signs. Whatever the reason, the prophet was not convinced by the king's shallow piety and his casual, even stubborn religious move that also happened to keep his own faith from being tested. "I will not ask!"

"Hear then, O house of David!" came the reply from Isaiah. When such an imperative is spoken by a prophet of the Lord, I take it to mean, "You better stand back and listen now!" "Hear then, O house of David! Is it too little for you to weary mortals, that you weary my God also?" In other words, "You can't settle for just wearing out the people around you — you have to wear God down as well? It isn't enough that your faithless waffling and the events that surround it so burden the heart of your people — you and the nations must also tug at the heart of God?" Therefore, Isaiah tells Ahaz, the Lord will give him a sign. God and God alone will give him a sign. "Look, the young woman is with child and shall bear a son, and shall name him Emmanuel." It was the sign that God was to give. This wearied God will give Ahaz a sign.

Maybe Matthew was right to say nothing about Ahaz. Maybe Matthew was on to something in saying to Advent preachers everywhere, "Let's not go there!" Advent and Christmas are a lot easier when you just lift the quote. In the six o'clock Monday morning Bible study here at the church, we started reading Isaiah at the beginning of Advent, figuring these familiar texts and phrases would carry our discussions leading up to Christmas. "Emmanuel" and "for unto us a Child is born" and "a shoot shall come out from the stump of Jesse" and "the ransomed of the Lord shall return and come to Zion with singing." So we started Isaiah. Our attendance immediately dropped. For almost the first time in two and a half years, the conversation struggled. "Too depressing," said one. "Too hard to understand," said another. "Not much to talk about" — and that came from me! We even tried pilfering some notes on lectures on Isaiah from the Introduction to the Old Testament class offered over at the seminary! It's all so much easier when this faith journey of ours, when our understanding of God and God's faithfulness, when our understanding of God and the world and the complexity of the nations, when it all fits on the front of a Christmas card!

But this sign — this sign comes dripping with humanity's history. This sign comes with the thickest of descriptions of God and God's people. This sign. It is a sign offered by a weary God in the midst of great fear and the world's tumult. It is a sign given even as the nastiness of the nations rages on and the endless talk and action of war overshadow any hope for peace. It is a sign that speaks even when an abundance of shallow piety and religion is used to justify and promote and entrench one's own selfish conclusions. It is a sign that comes despite humanity's pervasive skill in avoiding putting faith to the test. "I will not ask!"

You think Isaiah is depressing? You think Isaiah's too hard to understand? Remember that even when Matthew surgically removed that quote from Isaiah, the world's brutality came crashing in again when Herod had those children in and around Bethlehem slaughtered. The birth narrative itself resists being spiritually sanitized for our protection, for our enjoyment. Signs from a weary God. Look around! Look out this Advent. Look at the world! Behold! And then hear, O house of David. Isn't it enough this Advent that the hearts of all people must grow so weary? For God's sake, God must be weary too! Must we wear down the very heart of God? And yet . . . But . . . Alas . . . Even so . . . Still . . . Yet even then. Isaiah uses "Therefore." Therefore, the Lord will give you a sign.

A sign. Here this morning we have the Gospel words of promise and the baby and the water. A sign. The family is gathered around. The church presses in and snuggles yet again up to the font. Faith is confessed. Questions are answered. We invoke the Holy Spirit. And we observe the sign. We enact the sign. Water sprinkled. Just a bit of stream, hopefully to be seen from the farthest pew. Drops linger on the face of the child, in the hair, or trickle down the neck. It's a baptism Sunday. A sacramental Sunday consisting of "God's Word, of signs and of things signified, whereby in the Church God keeps in mind and from time to time recalls the great benefits God has shown to us" (Second Helvetic Confession, 1561). Sacred actions. Of signs and things signified.

We have sung "Gloria in Excelsis Deo." We have heard a Gospel reading from Matthew, from the birth narrative of Jesus. We are soon to share in "Hark! the Herald Angels Sing." Red flowers abound. Four candles are lit. This water-washing, this gathering down by the grace-filled river — it must be a Christmas baptism. A Christmas baptism. When the church comes to the font with freshened memories of the Christ Child swaddled, rocked, and nursed by Mary. When the church leans in to observe a washing, while pondering anew the Son of God born in flesh. The weight of glory revealed in five, maybe six pounds of fragile life. A Christmas baptism. When faith is confessed and questions are answered, all of it experienced in the light of God's promise of Emmanuel, God with us. A Christmas baptism, when you and I find ourselves struck, even wearied by tumultuous Advent, and so we squeeze in ever closer, holding on for dear life, yearning to see in this sacrament, in this sacred act, some assurance, some reminder, some inkling of God's greater sign. God with us. This sign forever framed by a greater sign.

Theologian Karl Barth was clear when it came to God's greater sign, the primary sacrament. At a public gathering of pastors, the conversation turned to liturgical questions, and Barth was asked to comment on the sacraments. Barth answered, "There is only one sacrament — the one who has himself risen from the dead." As Professor George Hunsinger describes Barth's thought here, Jesus Christ is the one true Word of God. Jesus Christ is the one true sacrament. The sign and the reality of grace so intertwined, so mutually related, so without separation or division. One sacrament. The bearer of grace. The embodiment of the promise. The Word made flesh. God with us.

One sign from God. Isaiah prodded Ahaz. Ask for a sign that plunges the very depths of hell. A sign that soars to the highest heavens. God's primary sign. It is Christ Jesus, crucified, raised from the dead, ascended to the throne of heaven. This sign. Born of Mary's womb. This flesh and blood he made holy. "Born that we no more may die, born to raise us from the earth, born to give us second birth." Sign. Reality. God with us.

We might have baptized Jesus this morning. I haven't thought about it before, but every year we must baptize Jesus sometime in the weeks leading up to the Christmas pageant. That church family drama where an unsuspecting infant is subject to the attention of robed shepherds and crowned Magi and a gaggle of children. The pageantry of God's promise will play itself out in chancels like this one in churches everywhere in the days to come. But before costumes and lights and staging, there is the font. Which is to say that the Christmas pageant doesn't begin when the star shines or when the manger is placed at center stage. It begins here at the font when a child is held in the church's arms and we again ponder the miracle of the Word made flesh. Not because of the cuteness of any one baby, not because of a casting call gone out, but because our weary God offers us this sign, where you and I gather with more than a bit of faith-filled hindsight and, with water dripping from our fingertips, we remember the great benefits God has shown to us. We remember and we celebrate and we witness and we live in and through God with us.

So you never hear much about Ahaz. But this time around, he struck me with his declaration: "I will not ask." So I offer a word for old Ahaz. Maybe it's because as this Advent comes to a close and the celebration of Christmas comes upon us, I don't know about you, but this time around, I need more than a sign. This week, may Emmanuel be born afresh for you, for us, for the world. God with us.

Born for This?

GALATIANS 3:23–4:7

⌒⁂⌒

I know it must have happened somewhere, in some church, during some Christmas pageant, sometime this afternoon or this evening. The pageant, as it unfolded — well, let's just say there were some significant kinks. Mrs. Wasley was only in her first year as the volunteer in charge, and if we're honest, it will probably be her last year. "Nightmare" would be too strong a word to ever use for a Christmas pageant. After all, the term "perfect Christmas pageant" is an oxymoron, a contradiction that flies in the face of the incarnation whereby God took on and made holy all of the frailty of this broken vessel of our humanity. Christmas pageants were made to have rough edges. However, this evening, as the pageant played on, Mrs. Wasley was just a bit taken aback by the sharpness of those edges.

Maybe there were a few things she would have done differently. For instance, maybe it wasn't such a good idea to have all the second and third graders be animals, especially after Billy McCallister asked if they could make animal noises, and Mrs. Wasley answered, "Yes, Billy, that might be very realistic." Or maybe somebody could have pointed out to Mrs. Wasley that it takes quite a bit of time to dress and move and fix the hair of the heavenly host, especially when it's made up of thirty-two angels all between two and four years old. And who would have thought that when working with the fifth-grade narrators, Taisha and Jerod, who were actually very fine readers, who would have thought that Mrs. Wasley would have wanted to go over punctuation with them?

Let's just say it was a rough afternoon in Bethlehem. Mary had been sick all morning, and the bucket next to the manger was for her to use. Joseph may have been a "righteous man and unwilling to expose Mary to public disgrace," but he was also thirteen and had decided about ten days ago that he wasn't going to enjoy this pageant at all. So Mrs. Wasley knew it was going to be a struggle. But when the animals arrived behind those shepherds, any hope of heavenly peace vanished. They took over the whole chancel and elevated "lowing" to a new cacophonous, hip-hop, rap-sounding art form. And the angels — well, the mom and dad working with the little angels backstage completely missed their cue, so the host arrived long after the wise men, even after the congregation had sung "Angels We Have Heard on High," even after the narrator Taisha had said four times, "And suddenly there was with the angel a multitude of the heavenly host." But when they finally arrived, they looked good: their halos were perfect, and their hair was all right.

But right near the end, right before everyone was to sing "Joy to the world! the Lord is come" and "He rules the world with truth and grace, and makes the nations prove the glories of his righteousness," right before the familiar Christmas hymn, the narrator Jerod fought his way to center stage for his last line. He stepped on and over an abundance of sheep and cows, even some dogs and cats and one child who came as a mouse. The angels' parents in the congregation were paying no attention to the narrator, making up for lost googling time and completely ignoring that request about flash pictures. Mary was reaching for the bucket, and Joseph had rolled his eyes so many times they just about fell out of his head. So Jerod had to shout over the barnyard noise, and he never did get the parents' attention. He put his folder down and stretched out his arms and with no small amount of exasperation yelled, "Christ was born for this??" And Mrs. Wasley, now fully exhausted, said to no one in particular, "It was an exclamation point, not a question mark."

Some years it feels more like a question mark, doesn't it? Christ was born for this? Some years, not the pageant as chancel drama, but this "rich pageant of life." That's how William Muehl once described it. "This rich pageant of life is often fouled up," he wrote. "Fouled up by our rigid moralism, and the cross is hidden beneath the flimsy fabric of our simple piety. . . . Our flesh drives and afflicts us from birth to death."[1] Christ was born for this? And you and I, we find ourselves stepping on and over, making our way across life's stage. Every year in this family of faith, somebody heads to Bethlehem by way of the grave. Death has an unceasing part to play. Every year, for some it is Christmas carols mixed with tears because the earthiness of the flesh has torn at relationships, or the brutality of disease has torn at the flesh. Christ was born for this? And this year, like every year, on the world's stage we come face to face with flesh not just torn but destroyed: destroyed by war, and nations proving something other than the "glories of his righteousness." We sing "peace on earth, goodwill to all" not just once or twice but over and over again, and still peace fails to make its entrance. Christ was born for this?

Have you ever noticed that Jesus seems to make the cover of *Time* and *Newsweek* fairly regularly? One of the managing editors once said in an interview that the best-selling cover stories have always been those on sex, religion, and science. This Christmas

1. William Muehl, *All the Damned Angels* (Philadelphia: Pilgrim Press, 1972), p. 13.

season alone, a few articles explored the birth narratives found in the Gospels of Luke and Mark: "Behind the First Noel. . . . How the Story of Christ's Birth Came to Be" and "The Birth of Jesus: From Mary to the Manger: How the Gospels Mix Faith and History to Tell the Christmas Story and Make the Case for Christ." The journalists engaged scholarly opinion to raise critical issues surrounding the Virgin Birth, and the importance of Bethlehem, and the numbers of the Magi, and whether or not the star was Halley's comet.

As I did my professional reading, I pondered how a popular magazine could make such discussions and the biblical research surrounding them sound so new. Christians have been wrestling with this material forever! And I came to the conclusion that the birth narratives, in and of themselves, as objects of study, don't bear the weight of salvation's story. When turning to the question of why this all makes a difference, both magazines looked to the message of the angel in Luke: "For to you is born this day in the city of David a Savior, who is Christ the Lord." "A simple, joyous proclamation of salvation," one writer concluded. "On earth peace, good will toward all," quoted the other writer, calling those words "a promise whose fulfillment is worth our prayers not only in this season, but always." A simple proclamation of salvation. A sweeping prayer for peace. As important as both may be, Christ was born for this? And the reader of *Time* or *Newsweek* ought to be turning pages looking for more, looking for what's missing, looking for why this Nativity of Christ would have anything to do with you or me.

Here's what's missing when the world chats about the Nativity. Christ came that you and I might be justified by faith. And "in Christ Jesus you are all children of God through faith." And "there is no longer Jew or Greek, there is no longer slave or free, there is no longer male and female; for all of you are one in Christ Jesus." That's what's missing. If you "belong to Christ, then you are Abraham's offspring, heirs according to the promise." This is what the

Apostle Paul writes in the Letter to the Galatians. It may not be cover-story material. But it is Paul's take on the birth of Jesus. "When the fullness of time had come, God sent his Son, born of a woman, born under the law, in order to redeem those who were under the law, so that we might receive adoption as children." No angels. No shepherds. No Magi. No star. But the fullness of time, and you and I as children of God. Christ was born for this!

The fullness of time. I don't have to call on the physicists among us to conclude that this fullness was not meant to be the end of the time line. That Paul must not have been talking about time in a linear way. Fullness. Complete. Almost perfect. Overflowing with grace. Just right. Fullness, as in "the earth is the LORD's and the fullness thereof" (RSV). Fullness, as in "I pray that you may have the power to comprehend with all of the saints, what is the breadth, and length, and height and depth, and to know the love of Christ that surpasses all knowledge, so that you may be filled with all the fullness of God." Fullness, as in "For in Christ, all the fullness of God was pleased to dwell." "When the fullness of time had come, God sent his Son, born of a woman."

I can remember Christmas Eve when I was a child. I sat in the pew next to my father. Every year we would sing "Silent Night," and the candlelight would spread, and my father would sing with tears streaming down his cheeks. The pew would even shake a bit. I used to say that on Christmas Eve my dad taught me that it was okay for men to cry. But my father taught me something much greater about faith and God's promises. Decades later, after more than our share of family pain, after months and months of twelve-step meetings every day, when he told me about his daily prayer life, about how he would quote Scripture in a prayer: "I can do all things through Christ who strengthens me." God's promise and the very earthiness of life. Such fullness of time belongs to God. Those moments when in the earthiness of our lives, you and I come face to face with the promise of God. The Nativity of the Christ Child in your life and in mine.

"I can do all things through Christ who strengthens me." (Phil. 4:13)

"I am convinced that neither death, nor life, nor angels, nor rulers, nor things present, nor things to come, nor powers, nor height, nor depth, nor anything else in all creation, will be able to separate us from the love of God in Christ Jesus our Lord." (Rom. 8:38-39)

"And remember, I am with you always." (Matt. 28:20)

"Peace I leave with you; my peace I give to you. I do not give to you as the world gives. Do not let your hearts be troubled, and do not let them be afraid." (John 14:27)

"Come to me, all you that are weary and are carrying heavy burdens, and I will give you rest. Take my yoke upon you, and learn from me; for I am gentle and humble in heart, and you will find rest for your souls." (Matt. 11:28-29)

"I am the bread of life. Whoever comes to me will never be hungry, and whoever believes in me will never be thirsty." (John 6:35)

"This is my body that is for you. Do this in remembrance of me." (1 Cor. 11:24)

Somewhere tonight in this rich pageant of life, somewhere a child of God is moving to center stage, stepping on and over, with more than an abundance of life's joys and challenges grasping at her feet. Few will pay attention, and she'll have to shout over the world's noise. But for her, it's the fullness of time. And with a heart stretched out to God, she will proclaim, not with a question mark but with an exclamation point, "Christ was born for this!"

Baptismal Consent

MATTHEW 3:13-17

On this early Sunday in January in our church, new officers were ordained, and elders and deacons came forward for a traditional laying on of hands.

A strange thing happened to me on the way to the pulpit this week. As I worked on this biblical text from the third chapter of the Gospel of Matthew, I realized I wasn't reading it alone. As I sat in my office, sat with Matthew's telling of the baptism of Jesus, I kept thinking of the three hundred or so of you who read this Scripture lesson with me. I am referring to those in the church family who have started to read through the Bible in a year. Matthew 3 was listed in last Monday's reading. A portion of Matthew 3:13-17 also happens to come in the assigned reading of the common lectionary for this Sunday after Epiphany, the Sunday in the liturgical calendar when the church hears again of the baptism of Jesus. And so on this last Monday morning, like most Monday mornings, I sat down with the sermon text for the week. But something strange was happening. You were reading it with me.

I guess it was about Thursday morning. The days of the week were rapidly disappearing. I was struggling with so familiar a text, struggling a bit in "putting together" a sermon. This so-familiar text: the Gospel's telling of the baptism of Jesus, and the heavens opening, and the Spirit descending like a dove, and a voice proclaiming, "This is my beloved Son" — if you didn't read it this week, you most likely know of it, the baptism of Jesus. So along about Thursday, with Sunday coming, and a most familiar text sort of dangling in my mind, and remembering this congregational effort in Bible-reading, I thought about calling you!

"Then Jesus came from Galilee to John at the Jordan, to be baptized by him." The familiar scene splashes on to the PowerPoint of our imagination. Along with it comes the familiar question, whether you're reading the passage for the first time or casually encountering a well-worn text: "Why would Jesus need to be baptized?" John's is a baptism of repentance and forgiveness of sins; a washing. Jesus, fully human, fully God, was tempted in every way, yet was without sin. So, no need to wash. Some would argue that the baptismal event was an anointing of Jesus as the Son of God. The Lord adopted Jesus at his baptism, making him then and there the very Son of God. "Adoptionism" is what they call it in the Christological debate through the centuries. However, the reader of Matthew's Gospel already knows of the child conceived of the Holy Spirit, and has read about the One named Jesus who will save his people from their sins, and has already come upon "Emmanuel," which means "God with us." According to Matthew, this child's identity as the Son of God comes long before Jesus "came up from the water." No Jordan River adoption here. So why would Jesus need to be baptized?

But it's still a Monday kind of question. It's a sort of first reaction; a first naiveté; a Monday-morning question of the biblical text. And it hangs around. So, somewhere amid a congregation of readers, somebody must have flipped quickly to Luke and Mark and John. Somebody must have gone searching for any further information about this baptism of Jesus. Was there any other twist? Any support for some other answers to the question? Answers like this one: Jesus' baptism offers something of a prototype, modeling for us the practice of baptism in the church. Or like this one: The baptism of Jesus is a public announcement offered to the crowds gathered on the riverbanks and to the Gospel readers and to the church. It is a coronation of sorts, an inauguration of public ministry, a divine affirmation that all of creation ought to now turn and watch. "This is my Son, the Beloved, with whom I am well pleased."

When you compare Matthew's narrative on the baptism of Jesus with the other Gospel narratives, it is the conversation between John and Jesus that stands out. It stands alone, only recorded in Matthew's Gospel. Only Matthew tells of this brief dialogue between the Baptist and the Son of God. Here's Matthew's answer to why Jesus was baptized: "John would have prevented him, saying, 'I need to be baptized by you, and do you come to me?' But Jesus answered him, 'Let it be so now; for it is proper for us in this way to fulfill all righteousness.' Then he [John] consented." Repentance for a sinless Messiah? Adoption there as the Son of God? A model for others to follow? A ritualized beginning to the Savior's ministry? The Monday-morning question about the baptism of the Lord in Matthew's Gospel. And Jesus said, "Let it be so now; for it is proper for us in this way to fulfill all righteousness."

Well, that clears that up! It is to fulfill all righteousness. Jesus was baptized by John in order to fulfill all righteousness — whatever that means. And so we roll up our theological sleeves and sharpen our pencils and get ready to hear and read and research the righteousness of God and the ministry of Christ as told by Matthew. It is a ministry that defines justice and mercy and compassion and obedience. Then we ponder that righteousness of Christ imputed to us through salvation's story of his life, death, and resurrection. And so we who are baptized in his name are called to a life of discipleship that somehow by God's grace seeks to reflect that fulfillment of all righteousness. On the occasion of our baptism, you and I are ordained to the ministry of Jesus Christ, a ministry that bears witness to God's salvation story. A ministry intended to fulfill all righteousness. Our theological machinations related to Jesus' baptism just keep churning. For the preacher, the Monday-morning question turns into Tuesday's homework and Wednesday's reading and Thursday's research. And with a complexity of language and some theological steam coming out of our ears, we are left to affirm that Jesus was baptized by John just because. Why? Because. A theological because. Valid, complex, warranted. Because. "Let it be so now; for it is proper for us in this way to fulfill all righteousness." Jesus said "because."

But back on Monday, when we first read the story of the baptism of Jesus here in Matthew, the actions seemed to speak louder than the words. The actions jumped off the page. Not just the actions of Jesus coming up from the water and the heavens cracking open and the Spirit descending and the voice booming. Even before all that, in what is unique Matthew, Matthew's answer to the question of why Jesus had to be baptized, even there in the encounter between John and Jesus, actions seemed to speak louder than words. Jesus came from Galilee to John to be baptized. John tried to prevent him. John said, "How and why?" Jesus said, "Because." And we read, "Then he consented." Then John consented. We had to read it a few times to make sure we got the pronouns straight. Then John consented to baptizing Jesus.

Christ himself is ordained for ministry as he entrusts himself to the arms of John. The Savior's work begins sacramentally, in the hands of another. But as John consented and baptized Jesus, it wasn't just the start of the Lord's ministry of teaching and healing and caring. It was the beginning of the church's ministry. It was the beginning of the church's service to Christ. It was the church seeing the face of Christ in the other. The church seeing Christ in the face of those entrusted to its care. With arms outstretched to the world, the church sees the very face of Christ. The church called to embody and proclaim God's love to the world. The church looking at the world and seeing Christ himself kneeling before us. John's baptismal consent. Jesus had to be baptized by John so that you and I could see the face of Christ in those we are called to serve, in one another, in the other. You and I, here indeed we are the body of Christ, but we dare not miss the face of Christ that kneels before us and awaits our care, awaits our service, awaits our ministry.

There never seems to be an end to the world's suffering. In any given week there are incomprehensible numbers of dead, orphaned children, people who have lost everything. And Christ is kneeling. There with the hungry and the thirsty and the sick and the naked and with the prisoners and the detainees and the immigrants defined as illegal. And even though the faith groups are so different from our own, and the faces so different, the people so different, do we not see the face of Christ there as well? You remember what Jesus said in Matthew about the hungry, the thirsty, the stranger, the naked, the sick, the prisoner. "As you did it unto them, you did it to me!" Christ before us. And in the church, on a Sunday of ordination and installation, it's important to remember that not all the baptized are welcomed here to be ordained. The way is blocked for some because of sexual orientation — an unfortunate blocking that I continue to lament. And in the midst of that painful churchly debate, it would seem we have long forgotten that even there, especially there in that conversation, it is the face of Christ we must see among those who stand before us, those who disagree with us. I'm not talking about that ethic of putting a name and a face with a conversation. I'm talking about putting the face of Christ in the midst of our service and ministry to the world.

So back on Monday morning, among these elders or deacons ordained and installed this morning, and among those to be ordained to office in the Presbyterian Church for the first time, among these folks called to leadership in Nassau Presbyterian Church, you read of the baptism of Jesus in the third chapter of Matthew's Gospel. I don't know if you noticed then, but you are standing with John and his baptismal consent. Serving Christ, that all righteousness might be fulfilled. By God's grace and in all of the wonder and promise of God's Spirit, I ask you, on behalf of all of us, to help us to embody God's love and to proclaim God's love and to witness to God's love here and just out there and in all the world. For when we stand together here in this churchly huddle of an ordination prayer, when we stand here and turn and look at the congregation, and through the door to the community and then to the world, it is the very face of Christ looking back at us.

Almighty

ISAIAH 44:1-8

A former professor at Princeton Seminary once described his experience of rising to say the Apostles' Creed in this sanctuary at Nassau Church. He stood next to his young son as the congregation affirmed faith using the familiar words. At some point during that particular recitation of the Creed, the theologian father realized that his son was saying every word. He also knew that the boy had not learned the Creed at home; he had learned it here at Nassau Church. Father and son, generation after generation, shoulder to shoulder, pew after pew. I believe in God the Father Almighty, Maker of heaven and earth.

"Now hear, O Jacob my servant, Israel whom I have chosen!" The Word of the Lord from the prophet Isaiah to the people of God struggling in exile — with homeland laid waste and reduced to barrenness, with a spiritual identity threatened daily by an abundance of idol worship that so surrounded them, with any sense of historical rootedness in God now lost in the chaos of life.

Into that desert of their existence, the prophet Isaiah speaks. "Thus says the LORD who made you, who formed you in the womb and will help you: Do not fear. . . . For I will pour water on the thirsty land, and streams on the dry ground." Thus says the Lord: "I am the first and I am the last; besides me there is no god. Who is like me? Let them proclaim it! . . . Do not fear, or be afraid. . . . You are my witnesses! Is there any god besides me? There is no other rock; I know not one." I will pour out my spirit on your descendants. My blessing will shower your children. They will thrive like trees next to a flowing stream, your children and your children's children. I will bring life out of this landscape of barrenness and desolation. "This one will say, 'I am the LORD's,' another will be called by the name of Jacob, yet another will write on the hand, "The LORD's." Your offspring, they shall rise and affirm that they "belong to the Living God who is like no other, whose promised creation is renewed in the fullness of our lives, indeed in the fullness of time, whose faithfulness is revealed in a hope-filled future that belongs to God alone. For there is no other rock, we know not one!"

I believe in God the Father Almighty, Maker of heaven and earth. You and I rise week in and week out. We struggle to our feet like weary travelers worn down by the landscape that so tries to define us. Our baptismal identities threatened by the abundance of idol worship that surrounds us. Any sense of certainty or assurance in God surely weather-worn and eroded by the world's confusion and life's chaos and the collective burdens carried in here every Sunday. And we stand together, generation after generation, parent and child, pew by pew, shoulder to shoulder. Offering a helping hand to one another to get up, occasionally tugging at one another, we say it with one another, we say it for one another, we say it for those who on any particular Lord's Day can't find voice. We find ourselves standing not so straight, yet standing with that great cloud of witnesses, the communion of saints, the choirs of heaven. I believe in God the Father Almighty, Maker of heaven and earth. Or how about this language: There is no other rock; we know not one! Or, for those used to writing notes on the hand: The Lord's! I am the Lord's! I believe in God the Father Almighty, Maker of heaven and earth.

You will not be surprised to learn that there is no shortage of theological material available on the Apostles' Creed in institutional libraries near here. Part of the scholarly tradition calls for systematic theologians to organize their work around and to write about the rule of faith: the Creed. So it would not be far-fetched to consider devoting our preaching life to dissecting every word, to exegeting every clause, to diagramming every sentence. We could easily spend five, maybe six weeks, or this whole season of Lent, on just this first article of the Creed. I believe in God the Father Almighty, Maker of heaven and earth. It is important work for the church, pondering the divine attributes. Like God as the Father of our Lord Jesus Christ, or the Almightiness of God, or God as the Creator. God, the One who shapes heaven not as the top floor of the cosmos, but as that which contains God's ultimate future. A future defined as God's hope for the earth. A future that reflects God's eternal creative breath. I believe in God the Father Almighty, Maker of heaven and earth.

In the church of Jesus Christ, where teaching and learning are far too often reduced to a twenty-minute sermon on Sunday, studying Christian doctrine has become something of a lost art. As we try to reclaim that art in our faith journey, a challenge comes when our theological homework collides with the landscape of our lives, or our intellectual capacity gets a bit full of itself and we think we have to know all the answers, or our postmodern arrogance concludes that of course we're further along than prior generations, or some question, some event, some natural disaster, some personal suffering rises up and demands an answer immediately.

Whenever we rise to say the Creed, maybe we should remember another father — not the one I first described, who stood here in this sanctuary, but the one described in the Gospel of Mark: the father who stood with his son before Jesus. What he wanted was for his son to be healed. "If you are able to do anything, have pity on us and help us!" Jesus said to him, "If you are able! — All things can be done for the one who believes." The father of the child cried out, "I believe; help my unbelief!" (Mark 9:22-24). And you and I, we stand up again and write on our hands: *The Lord's! I am the Lord's!* I believe in God the Father Almighty, Maker of heaven and earth! Or, in less religious language, perhaps in next-generation-friendly language, language yet biblical and pro-phetic: "There is no other rock! I know not one."

Our first graders and their parents shared in a class last week on communion education. Together they were preparing to come to the Lord's Table this morning. Perhaps like many of you, I did not participate in the sacrament of communion until I was con-firmed in the ninth grade. One of the reasons given then for the de-lay was that as children and young people we would not be able to understand what was going on. This implies, I guess, that grown-ups do understand all that goes on here at the Table — this visible sign of an invisible grace, this real presence of Christ, this eschato-logical banquet, this feast in the kingdom of heaven, this meal where we are made one with Christ and he with us. But that's just not the case. It's not the case that we grown-ups understand! Yet the feast goes on. Yet we feast on God's grace. *The Lord's! We are the Lord's!* It therefore feels right to me to begin our work with the Apostles' Creed, our Lenten discipline of catechetical preaching, to begin it here at the Table with every generation present. Here where words fail and grace pours out.

Ours is a tradition of creeds and confession. Ours is a tradi-tion of Word and Sacrament. Our faith lives and breathes some-where between the Creed and the Table. Which is all to say that I believe this first line of the Apostles' Creed is less about doctrinal perfection and more about identity formation. It says less about God than it does about us. For what we say about God is by defini-tion incomplete, unsatisfactory, never enough, never quite right. But when saying the Creed, we acknowledge that we are not God, that we, along with heaven and earth, are part of that which God has created, that which God continues to create. We stand as witnesses, those called out by the prophet Isaiah, offspring who have tasted a blessing, descendants who have received God's Spirit. "You are my witnesses! Is there any god besides me?" "There is no other rock! We know not one!" We belong to God and God alone! *The Lord's. We are the Lord's!* I believe in God the Father Almighty, Maker of heaven and earth.

The twentieth-century theologian Karl Barth was arguably one of the greatest minds the church has ever known. In his work with the Apostles' Creed, he warns of reducing it all to simply concepts and abstract ideas. It can't all be just an academic exercise. Barth's example comes with the almightiness of God! "God's almightiness is no abstract idea such as we often imagine when we say God 'can do everything,'" Barth writes. And he continues, "We fall then into ridiculous riddles: can God lie?" Such intellectual and theological gymnastics Barth describes as absurdities.

According to Barth, God's almightiness can be considered, discussed, made known only in the "exercise of the almightiness revealed to us in Jesus Christ." In Jesus Christ, God is hidden and reveals Godself. That is God's Almightiness. In Jesus Christ, God who is free and bound by nothing ultimately loves and binds Godself to that which God has created. That is God's Almightiness. God who is above all comes down below without ceasing to be sovereign. Almightiness. Or, as Barth so eloquently puts it, "In Jesus Christ, God, out of the mercifulness of his heart, comes down from eternity, before the world is created. God bears all sins, all miseries and even death. God wills to suffer in his Son, and bearing in him all our sins, he wills to glorify himself. Victorious through the Cross. That is God's Almightiness."[1] And we find

---

1. Karl Barth, *The Faith of the Church: A Commentary on the Apostles' Creed according to Calvin's Catechism,* edited by Jean Louis Leuber, translated by Gabriel Vahanian (New York: Meridian Books, 1958), p. 46.

ourselves right back at the Table, where God's Almightiness is made known afresh to us in the breaking of the bread and the pouring of the cup.

If we're honest about it, you and I will not soon give up talking about abstract ideas and pondering the attributes of God and engaging science and theology and trying to get a handle on tough questions and horrible events and natural disasters and random violence and the nature of evil. We're not going to stop trying to figure it all out. It's the human condition. Frankly, it's part of our call to faithfulness.

In the midst of this journey of faith, this quest for understanding, will you rise with me, as if to write again on your hand *The Lord's. I belong to the Lord*? Will you stand with me and proclaim, "There is no other rock. We know not one"? Will you rise with me and then come and taste of God's Almightiness? Will you stand with me and affirm our belonging? I believe in God the Father Almighty, Maker of heaven and earth!

Imprint

HEBREWS 1:1-5

In his foreward to a current volume of essays and sermons on the Apostles' Creed, Professor Geoffrey Wainwright from Duke Divinity School reveals a bit of "professorial humor." Whenever a student misplaces the apostrophe in writing the phrase "Apostles' Creed," when the student places the apostrophe in the wrong spot, putting it after the "e" instead of after the "s" in "Apostles," the professor then writes in the margin, "Which apostle?" The point, of course, is to affirm the church's ancient tradition about the Creed. The twelve Apostles, filled with the Holy Spirit, established this standard of faith before they were sent out to preach the gospel. Professor Wainwright points out that historically, each affirmation of the Creed was attributed to a particular Apostle, from Peter to Matthias, the replacement worker for Judas. Thus, the collective connotation of implied authorship signaled by the properly placed apostrophe is not to be missed when it comes to the Apostles' Creed.[1]

1. Geoffrey Wainwright, foreword to *Exploring and Proclaiming the Apostles' Creed*, edited by Roger E. Van Harn (Grand Rapids: William B. Eerdmans Publishing Company, 2004), p. ix.

Frankly, the work of the late theologian Shirley Guthrie is more convincing here on what is known about the origins of the Creed. He simply sums it up. It is attributed by legend to those first twelve. It is more likely a baptismal creed used in Rome in the second century. The present form is not found before the sixth or seventh century.[2] It is one of the most ancient and ecumenical of Christian creeds used primarily in the tradition of the Western church. This morning, it is the second article of the Creed that awaits our consideration: "I believe in Jesus Christ, his only Son, our Lord."

I know this probably sounds strange to you, coming from me, but when I stop and think about it, I am always amazed by the number of conversations I have about Jesus. Now mind you, they fall across a vast spectrum that includes cocktail-party and soccer-field conversations I would just as soon avoid. And there have been other memorable kinds of encounters over the years. Almost twenty years ago a very old church member told me she was absolutely convinced that Jesus came and sat on the edge of her tub while she was in the bath. About fifteen years ago a clinical social worker at the hospital very convincingly explained to me that she could allow me to visit with the parishioner hospitalized because of schizophrenia only if I promised not to mention the name of Jesus. About twelve years ago a young woman dying from cancer told me that Jesus had come to her room the night before. And just last year, when a Jewish neighbor invited me to a local temple's adult education discussion on "what Jews think about Jesus," the honest answer came from one corner: "I don't think anything. Growing up I just didn't think about Jesus at all." And then there is the disagreement I had just two weeks ago with some colleagues during a theological examination on the floor of presbytery — it was about a candidate's understanding of Jesus as the way to salvation.

All this talk about Jesus. It's hard to keep track of it. But this

2. Shirley C. Guthrie Jr., *Christian Doctrine* (Louisville: Westminster John Knox, 1994), p. 32.

morning I'm thinking of the really important, deeply felt, intellectually challenging, honestly searching, life-giving and life-forming, one-on-one foundational kinds of conversations that I have again and again about Jesus. Conversations I have with you: about belief, about resurrection, about divinity, about the heavenly Christ, about the Trinity, about Jesus in a pluralistic age. About a relationship with Jesus lost, a relationship found. The more I talk with you about Jesus, the more I come to understand that the church has done you a disservice. I don't mean this church in particular, but the church tradition. Because more often than not I speak with people who have been led to believe that they are the only ones who have doubts, or who wrestle with questions, or who are willing to ask about really important stuff, or who dare to wonder when it comes to this Jesus.

The truth is, Christians have been trying to understand Jesus since the day the Lord put Peter on the spot: "Who do you say that I am?" Since the time John penned that prologue to his Gospel, offering a profoundly philosophical take on the Incarnation: "And the Word became flesh and lived among us, and we have seen his glory, the glory as of a father's only son, full of grace and truth." Since the preacher in the Letter to the Hebrews stood up and began to speak: "Long ago God spoke to our ancestors in many and various ways by the prophets, but in these last days God has spoken to us by a Son, whom God appointed heir of all things, through whom God also created the worlds. He is the reflection of God's glory and the exact imprint of God's very being."

In every century, in every generation, the greatest theological minds, the most faithful of souls — not just one or two out on the fringe labeled as skeptic, not just the ones history calls heretics, but a great cloud of witnesses, those who know themselves to be followers — they have been trying to figure it out. They have been willing to ask; they have learned to be honest about wrestling with the identity of Jesus, God's only Son, our Lord!

My hunch is that's because life happens. The questions keep

coming, the doubts are made more real, and the conversations about Jesus multiply because amid our ivory-tower search for answers, life happens. Children grow. Parents die. Joy abounds. Tragedy strikes. Love sparks. Relationships fail. Walls come down. The world shrinks. Interfaith dialogue is no longer a world council — it's a third-grade class. Genocide takes shape again. New alliances give hope. Disease breaks out. Wars never cease. The market rises and falls. Presidents come and go. What was once the world's next generation now rock their grandchildren to sleep. Through it all, the church and its academy engage the Christological questions. And you and I keep talking about Jesus. Not because we can't get the answers right, but because every Sunday's recitation of the Apostles' Creed is a bit different! Every Sunday's affirmation is a living, breathing witness to our faith. Every Sunday, from the pastoral realities and the incredibly complex web of conversation that define our life as a community, we stand with John and his Gospel, we stand with the preacher in this Letter to the Hebrews, we stand with the Apostles, and we point to Jesus Christ, God's only Son, our Lord.

John Polkinghorne, a scientist and theologian, spoke of this fragile, creedal pointing to Christ in his Gifford Lectures a decade ago. At one point he was speaking about understanding Christ and the use of the various titles of Jesus. Polkinghorne suggested that the church's use of such titles ought to be compared to the use of models in science. Scientists know that such models are useful but limiting. Models are intended to be exploratory and heuristic, not exhaustive. Scientists fruitfully engage models knowing they must be used with a "considerable degree of tolerance of unresolved difficulty."[3] Creedal affirmations and scientific models?

3. John Polkinghorne, *The Faith of a Physicist: Reflections of a Bottom-Up Thinker: The Gifford Lectures for 1993-94* (Princeton: Princeton University Press, 1994), p. 130.

Polkinghorne points out that questions of Christology arise not from speculation but from experience (not because we can't get it right, but because life happens!). When the church rises to speak about Jesus, Polkinghorne concluded, it has less to do with thoughts and ideas about him, and more to do with our experience of him. The church rising to affirm faith, not with fingers crossed until we've figured it all out, but with fingers pointing to the One we yearn to know and to understand and to proclaim: Jesus Christ, God's Son, our Lord. Our collective affirmation — God knows it is far from free of doubt; God knows we have yet to fully understand the things of this Jesus; God knows on any particular Lord's Day there are those in here who can't say a word of it; God knows there are theological questions from these pews that dare to approach anger and lament. And yet "we declare to you what was from the beginning, what we have heard, what we have seen with our eyes, what we have looked at and touched with our hands, concerning the word of life" (1 John 1:1).

In a recent essay published in *Theology Today*, Professor Patrick Miller offers an intriguing argument about a missing clause here in the Creed. He suggests that we should begin, "I believe in God the Father Almighty, Creator of heaven and earth, who delivered Israel from Egyptian bondage." It is a convincing argument he makes about understanding the Christian faith with a lens properly focused on the Old Testament canon. Miller's adjustment in focus also deepens our understanding of the liberating work of Christ. Right at the beginning of his article, Dr. Miller suggests that one function of the Creed is that it informs Christian interpretation and the reading of Scripture. While the Creed is not intended to represent the full scriptural witness, Miller writes, "the creed intends to get to the heart of the matter." I read Miller here as encouraging the double meaning when it comes to "the heart of the matter." The Creed is intended to speak to the very core, the very center of Christian faith. And the Creed is more than just an intellectual summary. It reflects something of the heart when it comes to Christian faith. Not just speculation, but experience.[4]

Talk of Jesus is talk of the One who is the reflection of God's glory. The exact imprint of God's very being. This Jesus, who touched the unclean and knelt to embrace the sinner and chose to dine with the least religious one he could find. This Jesus, who dared to speak to a foreign woman there at the well, who found himself duly challenged, even chastised by another who demanded table crumbs for the well-being of her daughter, who even chose to teach Mary and Martha in a culture that no doubt believed that women were created different from men and were not able to learn theology. This Jesus, who turned matters of the law into matters of the heart, who placed the concern for the individual above the celebration of the Sabbath, who defined servant-leadership long before the *Harvard Business Review*. This Jesus, who exhibited a divine nonviolence that ought to forever change our understanding of God and of us, who engaged interfaith dialogue in something other than a triumphalistic and conquering way, who challenged understandings of money and power and religious practice far more than anything we try to define as family values. This Jesus who shed tears and showed anger and sweated blood and found himself abandoned there on the cross with broken bones and a broken heart. This Jesus is the exact imprint of God's very being.

If I were keeping score during my almost twenty years of ministry, I would say that much of the questioning I've encountered has been about the divinity of Jesus. But as I look out at the world, your world and mine, and see the unique challenges of international politics, interfaith dialogue, and an increasing desire among people of faith to be right all the time, I am increasingly convinced that it is time to be struggling to comprehend the hu-

4. Patrick Miller, "Rethinking the First Article of the Creed," *Theology Today,* January 2005, pp. 499-508.

manity of God. Maybe I can't fully comprehend what is meant when the heavenly voice proclaims, "You are my Son, today I have begotten you" (Heb. 5:5). But tears and suffering and a broken heart? He is the exact imprint of God's very being.

I guess we're going to have more conversations, aren't we? More conversations about Jesus.

Suffering

MATTHEW 16:13-28

━━━━

"Who was conceived by the Holy Ghost, born of the Virgin Mary, suffered under Pontius Pilate, was crucified, dead, and buried." I must confess that I feel a bit like a child who winds his way through a cafeteria line with eyes much bigger than his tummy. Everything looks good and worthy of a spot on his tray. Parental supervision is somewhat lacking, so he loads it up. Jell-O. Chicken fingers. French fries. A bit of salad. Mac and cheese. A slice of pizza. A bag of chips. Less than twenty minutes later, the tray is full of half-eaten portions. Far too much is wasted. Nothing looks as good as it did before, and it doesn't taste as good either. It's a developmental thing, I guess. Kids and cafeteria lines. Eventually eyesight and healthy portions and disciplined choices have to come into play.

I imagine some of you have heard more than your share of sermons that sort of sounded like that tray looked. Twenty minutes in and full of half-eaten portions, half-baked ideas. Too much wasted. Preachers, too, ought to learn about healthy portions and disciplined choices when it comes to sermon fare! Which is my way of saying that if you were expecting a sermon on the Virgin Birth this morning, you are about to be disappointed. Choices must be made. As implied in this sermon title and communicated by the Scripture lesson from Matthew, I have had to limit what goes on the plate.

It seems to me, however, that "conceived by the Holy Ghost, born of the Virgin Mary" is less about biology and more about the identity of Jesus, which happened to fill our sermonic plate last week. This particular creedal couplet that affirms Jesus as fully God and fully human — perhaps it is the period to last week's sermon rather than the pick-up note to this week's. It is a formulaic expression of God's ultimate revelation: Jesus Christ, God's only Son, our Lord. The Nicene Fathers said it this way: "God from God, light from Light, true God from true God, begotten, not made, of one Being with the Father. . . . He came down from heaven, was incarnate of the Holy Spirit and the Virgin Mary, and became truly human."

More than thirty years ago, theologian Wolfhart Pannenberg mused that most Christians would probably "look for a different way of expressing God's intention from the one offered by the story of the Virgin Birth." Pannenberg defines God's intention as "that unique revelation made known in Jesus of Nazareth, who was, and is, in his person from the very beginning the only Son of God, humankind's mediator of the sovereignty of God."[1] "Conceived by the Holy Ghost, born of the Virgin Mary." Spirit. Birth. Divinity. Humanity. A creedal reference to the two natures of Christ.

You can cross your arms and huff when it comes to the Virgin Birth, or you can stand with the faithful in every age yearning to encounter what the Apostle Paul describes as "the fullness of time." As he writes in Galatians, "But when the fullness of time had

---

1. Wolfhart Pannenberg, *The Apostles' Creed in the Light of Today's Questions*, translated by Margaret Kohl (Philadelphia: Westminster Press, 1972), p. 77.

come, God sent his Son, born of a woman, born under the law" (4:4). If you're expecting the Creed to explain what cannot be explained, you will also be disappointed long after this morning's sermon. As Karl Barth points out, "We do not pretend to explain, and besides, neither did the Councils [who authored such creeds] nor the Reformers [like Luther, Calvin, and Zwingli]. Like them, we want to convey the event which is the union, the Covenant, of God and humankind in Jesus Christ and which itself is a mystery."[2]

A mystery. An encounter. An event. An experience. The story of Jesus Christ, God's only Son, our Lord, "conceived by the Holy Ghost, born of the Virgin Mary, suffered under Pontius Pilate, was crucified, dead, and buried."

There in the sixteenth chapter of the Gospel of Matthew, in the rather familiar exchange between Jesus and Peter, the Apostle is confronted with the question of the identity of Jesus. The Gospel narrative tells of Peter's attempt to understand the Messiah, the Son of the living God. When Peter gets to the suffering part in the throes of his relationship with Jesus of Nazareth, as Peter goes nose-to-nose with this identity of Jesus, just as Peter gets to the suffering, that's when Matthew tells us that Peter "took Jesus aside and began to rebuke him, saying 'God forbid it, Lord! This must never happen to you.'" When Peter got to the suffering part, he refused to hear it. So, predictably for Peter, he denied it. He questioned it. He wanted no part of it.

Every time the church stands to say and hear the Apostles' Creed, you and I are confronted by the identity of Jesus. When we get to the suffering, we just speed up, rush by it. Certainly we don't rebuke it, but we ignore it if we can! "Suffered under Pontius Pilate, was crucified, dead, and buried." When it comes to the life of Jesus in the Apostles' Creed, there isn't much there anyway. From

2. Karl Barth, *The Faith of the Church: A Commentary on the Apostles' Creed according to Calvin's Catechism*, edited by Jean Louis Leuber, translated by Gabriel Vahanian (New York: Meridian Books, 1958), pp. 82-83.

the Virgin Birth to the crucifixion, there's not much in between. So just push on by "suffered under Pontius Pilate." If you take a breath in the wrong place, you'll miss it.

But the suffering begins before the crucifixion. In both the Creed and the teaching of Jesus to his disciples about his own Passion, in both, suffering happens before the crucifixion. Jesus says that he must "undergo great suffering at the hands of the elders and chief priests and scribes." The Creed says, "Suffered under Pontius Pilate." As the Roman Catholic author Joan Chittister suggests, "The Creed requires us to remember the suffering that preceded the death itself." In but a phrase, the Creed places the Lord's suffering within the wide perspective of his entire life. Or, as Chittister puts it, "The outpouring of divine self that came moment by mundane moment all the years before . . . Jesus' death is not distinct from who he was, from what he was doing before the arrest, the mock trial, the rejection by the crowds. . . . Jesus suffered far greater pains than death long before death was kind enough to take him." She concludes, "There was more to the purpose of his life than a Roman cross. It was the life he lived that led to the cross upon which he died."[3] Or, as others have put it, the suffering of Jesus really began at his Nativity.

My intent here is not to elongate or elevate suffering for suffering's sake, nor am I intending to take away from the unique God-forsakenness that struck Jesus there upon the cross at Calvary's hill (that too would be another sermon). But I am suggesting that the phrase "suffered under Pontius Pilate" is worthy of a stretch. For that which he suffered under Pontius Pilate started long before. It started when Mary sang about the Mighty One who "has brought down the powerful from their thrones, and lifted up the lowly" (Luke 1:52); when Joseph took the child and his mother and fled to Egypt because the powerful knew then to be threat-

---

3. Joan Chittister, *In Search of Belief* (Liguori, Ill.: Liguori/Triumph, 1999), pp. 104-5.

ened, and Herod slaughtered the innocents; when Jesus read from the scroll, "The Spirit of the Lord is upon me, because he has anointed me to bring good news to the poor. He has sent me to proclaim release to the captives and recovery of sight to the blind, to let the oppressed go free, to proclaim the year of the Lord's favor" (Luke 4:18-19).

From the ark of Mary's womb to the moment Pilate's words — "Behold the man!" — fell upon his ears, Jesus suffered under Pontius Pilate. The uniqueness of his humanity, his unquenchable desire to love, and his never-ending fountain of grace — all of it, all of him, from before day one. He was shunned and rejected by the powers and principalities, by the world, by the kingdoms of this earth. He suffered under Pontius Pilate. With the nature of his self-giving compassion, with the depth of his self-emptying sacrifice, with the unrelenting way in which he cared for the other, with his self-denying, being-last-in-order-to-be-first, being-servant-of-all approach to life, he never had a chance. He suffered under Pontius Pilate.

After Jesus rebuked Peter right back — remember "Get behind me, Satan!"? — after Jesus rebuked Peter right back and labeled his waffling on suffering as a stumbling block, Jesus turned to his disciples and said, "If any want to become my followers, let them deny themselves and take up their cross and follow me. For those who want to save their life will lose it, and those who lose their life for my sake will find it." After the brief Ph.D. seminar on the identity of Jesus, the Lord turned to those who followed him, and the talk turned to discipleship. He didn't expect them to fully comprehend his unique suffering and death. He knew they couldn't understand it. After all, he told them not to tell. Jesus didn't turn to his disciples and offer a one-semester course on ways to understand his suffering and death, a course listed in the catalog as "Atonement Theory: From Sacrifice to Ransom to Substitution." Jesus didn't offer further detail or physical descriptions of his own suffering that would invite their reflection.

No. Jesus turned and told his disciples about self-giving compassion, and self-emptying sacrifice, and self-denial, and the last being first and being servant of all. Jesus turned to those who would follow him, to all who would take the name of Christian, he turned and told them he expected them to do the same, to live a life completely antithetical to the expectations of the world, and the powers that be, and the kingdoms of this earth. After being confronted with the identity of the Messiah, the Son of the living God, in the Gospel of Matthew, Peter and the rest of the disciples were told to follow Jesus. Jesus called them to a life of servanthood. They were being called to deny themselves and take up their cross and follow. Jesus was calling them to suffer under Pontius Pilate.

My guess is that you and I will never fully comprehend, at least on this side of glory, the unique suffering and saving death of Christ. For some in our congregation, such an endeavor is a life's work in service to Christ and his church. For others, trying to understand how it all works remains a stumbling block to faith. And no doubt the rest of us fall somewhere in between. But in the meantime, Christ is calling each one of us to a life of servanthood that comes with the freedom to turn from the world's way to the joy that comes in living for him. The Lord's charge to us couldn't be more clear.

To be honest, I've never really thought much about Pontius Pilate and his reserved parking spot here in the Apostles' Creed right next to the Virgin Mary. Maybe Pilate stands there to remind me, to remind us, of the life of discipleship in Christ to which we have all been called. For, like Pilate, we stand with both feet firmly planted in this world, with all of its trappings and with all of its power, and the living Christ stands before us asking, "Who do you say that I am?"

"If any want to become my followers, let them deny themselves and take up their cross and follow me."

Sheol

PSALM 139:1-12

In the Presbyterian church of my childhood and youth out there in Pittsburgh, I grew up singing from the red hymnbook published in 1955 and edited by David Hugh Jones. I'm actually speaking rather literally when I say that "I grew up singing from the hymnbook." My memories of it run deep. Hymn #1 is "Praise Ye the Lord, the Almighty, the King of Creation." Hymn #2 is "For the Beauty of the Earth." Advent comes in the 140's. Easter is right around 200. The congregation I served down in South Jersey used the red hymnbook. I will always remember that on one of the front pages, before the hymns even start, there are some prayers listed, and the creeds, Nicene and Apostles'. In the printed version of the Apostles' Creed, there is an asterisk. It comes right after the phrase "He descended into hell." The annotation reads, "Some churches omit this."

Several years ago I listened to a student's sermon prior to his preaching it on a Sunday morning in the congregation where he was doing his fieldwork. While I don't remember the exact words he used, at some point in his sermon he mentioned that God did not abandon Jesus on the cross. As we talked about the sermon afterward, I said something like, "But you know that's exactly what God did — God abandoned Jesus on the cross." We talked about what the tradition labels the cry of dereliction: "My God, my God, why hast thou forsaken me?" Our conversation lasted for awhile, became a bit animated. The student disagreed with me. He held his own preaching ground and didn't change a word of his sermon. We were arguing about "He descended into hell." Some churches omit this.

One preacher wrote an essay in which he described the reaction from a member of the congregation when the subject came up: "My Jesus did not descend into hell!"[1] Of course that preacher is every preacher, and every congregation includes those who would firmly hold to what that member said. Jesus, "God's only Son, our Lord, who was conceived by the Holy Ghost, born of the Virgin Mary, suffered under Pontius Pilate, was crucified, dead, and buried." This same Jesus who was tempted in every way, yet was without sin, who could not in any way, shape, or form experience the burning, wrath-filled depths of eternal punishment and damnation. "My Jesus did not descend into hell!" My hunch is that every Sunday morning in a typical congregation like this one, when we are reciting the Creed and we get to "He descended into hell," some parts of the church omit this. A tainted creedal affirmation forever listed in the record book with an asterisk — at least in the red hymnbook.

Speaking of a hymnbook, the psalmist is singing this morning. The singing comes from the words of Psalm 139 that I read to you just a moment ago. These words and images and affirmations of the psalmist — the memories run deep for people of faith, very deep. "Where can I go from your spirit? Or where can I flee from

---

1. Scott Black Johnston, "Harrowing," in *Exploring and Proclaiming the Apostles' Creed*, edited by Roger E. Van Harn (Grand Rapids: William B. Eerdmans Publishing Company, 2004), p. 132.

your presence? If I ascend to heaven, you are there; if I make my bed in Sheol, you are there. If I take the wings of the morning and settle at the farthest limits of the sea, even there your hand shall lead me, and your right hand shall hold me fast." The psalmist is singing.

Sometimes the song of the psalmist strikes an even deeper chord. You remember this one: "Yea, though I walk through the valley of the shadow of death, I will fear no evil, for thou art with me; thy rod and thy staff, they comfort me" (KJV). I grew up singing from that hymnbook too. When I walk through the valley of the shadow of death, thou art with me. When I make my bed in Sheol, thou art with me. No churches omitting here! Psalm 23. Psalm 139. No asterisk here.

One of my teachers, James Kay, has written a very helpful essay that rehearses just a bit of the history of Christian thought on the phrase "He descended into hell." Professor Kay gives an explanation that might be added to the "asterisk file" on the Creed. This descension clause was a late addition to the Creed; "hell" never made it into the earlier drafts. Kay suggests that "hell enters the creed" as an exclamation point on the death of Jesus.[2] He was dead, really dead. He went to Sheol, the place of the dead. He was dead and buried and descended into hell. It is like the Church Fathers affirming he was dead, dead, dead. DEAD. Dead. Dead. Dead. You can guess the logic here. A strong proclamation of the resurrection of Jesus Christ is rather dependent upon the certainty of his death, made ever more certain by underlining his dwelling place there among the dead, there in Sheol.

In addition to the man I mentioned above who told the preacher he couldn't settle for Jesus being in hell, I bet every congregation includes a searching and inquiring member who has read a little ahead in the Bible. So she embodies (in my imagina-

---

2. James F. Kay, "He Descended into Hell: *Descendit ad inferna*," in *Exploring and Proclaiming the Apostles' Creed*, pp. 117-29.

tion at least) everyone who has ever asked the pastor for the biblical support for such confession. "Where does it say in the Bible that he descended into hell?" One answer comes in the Epistle of 1 Peter 3:18-20: "Christ was put to death in the flesh, but made alive in the spirit, in which also he went and made a proclamation to the spirits in prison, who in former times did not obey." Christ is the guest preacher in the house of the dead, preaching Good News and liberating those who went to the grave long before. Preaching to a captive audience, not simply those who had never heard, but those who had disobeyed, those intended for the wrath of God. According to 1 Peter, Christ descended in order that the gospel might be proclaimed even to the dead.

My pastoral experience here informs me that many folks listen respectfully to that bit of biblical support from 1 Peter and squint a bit, maybe cock their heads, and then wait for a bit more theological nourishment to chew on, having been left rather unsatisfied by the passing biblical argument. Don't worry! We're in good company here. The likes of John Calvin and Martin Luther didn't appear to be overly excited about 1 Peter either. For Martin Luther, Christ's descent was the mental anguish he endured upon the cross, his agony of conscience — to so fully understand the nearness of God and yet to be so far removed from God. Like Luther, John Calvin wasted little time on pondering hell as some place several floors below. He saw Christ's descent into hell as his suffering there on the cross. This physical suffering in view of all was combined with an invisible suffering whereby Christ himself endured the torment of condemnation. The one who is without sin experienced the severity of God's wrath on behalf of sinners all.

"He descended into hell." It's not an exclamation point intended to affirm that Christ really died. It's an arrow that points not downward but to what Paul described as the breadth and length and height and depth. He descended into hell. It points to the extent of Christ's suffering, to the love of Christ that surpasses all knowledge — a suffering and a love that, of course, can't be fully explained.

According to the Reformers, the challenge of wrapping your mind and faith around Christ's descent into hell comes not in the mythology of space (he plunged the depths), or in the tyranny of a timeline (the cross on Good Friday, hell on Saturday, resurrection on Sunday), or in the search for the right biblical proof text (1 Peter 3), but in the enormity of the theological point being made. For you cannot fully grapple with salvation's story, or with Christ's atoning sacrifice on the cross; you cannot really work on a theology of death and resurrection weather-worn by the experiences and realities of this life, or encounter an honest notion of the suffering that persists in this world, suffering that confounds even the heart of God; you cannot really hear a preacher stand at a memorial service and say that death shall not have the last word here and then listen at the cemetery as she reads from 1 Corinthians, "Death has been swallowed up in victory. Where, O death, is your victory? Where, O death, is your sting?"; you cannot fully confront your relationship with a God who walks with you in the valley of the shadow of death and with a God who rests with you when you make your bed in Sheol — you cannot do it without allowing your heart to be gripped and squeezed by the idea that there at the cross Jesus Christ went straight to hell. As Dr. Kay summarizes Calvin here, "Hell in the Creed is defined by the cross of Jesus Christ. Hell is godforsakenness." Or, in Calvin's own words, hell is "to feel yourself forsaken, and estranged from God, and when you call upon God, not to be heard."[3] "He descended into hell." You can't omit this!

I grew up singing from that red hymnbook, and I grew up singing along with the psalmists. When I was in third grade, my oldest brother was killed in a car accident. I remember sitting outside in the backyard that spring morning after the news had

---

3. Kay, "He Descended into Hell," p. 125.

come, as the pastor came, family arrived, the church gathered. And I remember hearing my mother cry. Her lament went right through the walls of the house, and it went on for a long time. Years later she told me how angry she got when people told her it must have been God's will. But she also told me how angry she was at God, how she would have it out with God on her knees — not in prayer at first, but when she was on her knees scrubbing the basement floor. The strokes with a brush became shouts. The cleaning water mixed with tears. I am forever grateful for her honesty of faith, for her willingness to show her children something of her relationship to God, for testifying to her encounter with Jesus smack in the midst of her experience of god-forsakenness. For helping me to see what happens when "He descended into hell" and "Yea, though I walk through the valley of the shadow of death" — to see what happens when those songs meet.

That's why I say it. When silence falls after the robust theological conversation, when our attempts to figure it all out are done for yet another day, when this doctrinal sermon comes to a close, I will say it because it's part of my growing-up faith. "He descended into hell." I say it because "I am convinced that neither death, nor life, nor angels, nor rulers, nor things present, nor things to come, nor powers, nor height, nor depth, nor anything else in all creation, will be able to separate us from the love of God in Christ Jesus our Lord" (Rom. 8:38-39). Because when I walk through the valley of the shadow of death, God promises to walk with me. I say it because there is nowhere I can go to flee from God's presence. "If I ascend to heaven, you are there; if I make my bed in Sheol, you are there. If I take the wings of the morning and settle at the farthest limits of the sea, even there your hand shall lead me, and your right hand shall hold me fast."

At the end of his essay on this phrase from the Creed, James Kay concludes, "There is absolutely no possibility for us and for all creation that is beyond the reach of the triune God's unfathomable, unquenchable, and irresistible love."[4] I believe that. And so I say, "He descended into hell." And the next time I find myself standing next to a hospital bed when doctor's reports couldn't be worse, or walking into a living room full of unspeakable grief, or gathering with you here when the world's reality has come crashing in — the next time you and I find ourselves clinging to not much more than this growing-up faith, I'm going to read from Romans 8, and I'm going to read Psalm 139, and I'm going to read Psalm 23. Not because it is simply what you do with this office, not because I will have nothing else to say (though that indeed may be true). We will read it and proclaim it together because "He descended into hell."

4. Kay, "He Descended into Hell," p. 129.

Coming

ACTS 1:6-11

⟡

This morning is the fifth Sunday of Lent, and I think some reminders would be helpful. For those of you who may not know, there is some intention to our Lenten disciplines here at Nassau Church. The fellowship that we shared around the Lord's Table on Ash Wednesday and on the first Sunday of Lent has spread throughout our community as folks have joined in homes and shared communion with a common liturgy. The encounter with Scripture continues as several hundred in our church family journey along in the "Year of the Bible" daily reading. Educational opportunities in understanding the sacraments and in exploring our vocation as followers of Christ provide occasions for reflection and serve to remind us that the Lenten pathway is far from an individualistic spiritual exercise.

The core of these plans, the center of this web of discipline, I would suggest to you, has been the corporate worship of the people of God on the Lord's Day. Some intentional threads are woven here as well. Worship leadership that has included children, youth, and college and seminary students. An approach to confession that has included more silence for prayer, less words, and more music. A psalm of the day read or sung. A hymn differently placed. All of it intended not to throw you off your game (you Presbyterians who don't like change in worship), not to add more singing for singing's sake, but to set apart, to bracket, to frame our Lenten worship. To both set apart and then establish continuity week to week as together here, as a community of faith, we would journey with Christ Jesus in a season of penitence, reflection, and discipline.

The week-to-week connection has included our preaching life, as we have been working our way through the Apostles' Creed. A Lenten study of the Creed, attention offered to doctrine during the season, resonates with the most ancient practices of the Christian church. This morning we arrive here: "On the third day he rose again from the dead. He ascended into heaven, and sitteth on the right hand of God the Father almighty. From thence he shall come to judge the quick and the dead." You understand, of course, that we will hold off on the resurrection — that's just two weeks from now. So our Scripture lesson and sermon text come from the Acts of the Apostles 1:6-11.

"Then Jesus led them out as far as Bethany, and, lifting up his hands, he blessed them. While he was blessing them, he withdrew from them and was carried up into heaven. And they worshiped him, and returned to Jerusalem with great joy; and they were continually in the temple blessing God." Those are the very last verses of the Gospel of Luke. A rather succinct description of "He ascended into heaven." Luke's Gospel, his missive written to Theophilus, the lover of God, continues in book two, the Acts of the Apostles. The informed reader of the New Testament who makes the connection between Luke and Acts and therefore takes a temporary pass on the Gospel of John in order to read Luke-Acts together — he or she can't help but notice the reprise of the Ascension found in the first several verses of Acts. It is a reprise that offers a bit more flesh to those narrative bones. The risen Christ has now been with the disciples for forty days. This scene includes a bit of dialogue between Jesus and the disciples. There is a question about a time line, a promise of the Holy Spirit, a commissioning to the "ends of the earth." In Luke's second Ascension, "the cloud" takes a part. The cloud — always an appropriate biblical symbol — plays a role that affirms the presence of the divine, a part that reflects something of God's holiness. And Luke's revisiting of the Ascension includes the two men in white robes who appear as the followers of Jesus stand staring up toward heaven. "Men of Galilee, why do you stand looking up toward heaven? This Jesus, who has been taken up from you into heaven, will come in the same way as you saw him go into heaven."

Elder Beverly Gaventa notes the differences between Luke's two Ascension accounts in her commentary on Acts. The Gospel conclusion, in its crisp narrative, focuses on Jesus himself. The Acts preface, the Ascension story with just a bit more detail, offers a turn to the community of believers identified, established, and commissioned by Jesus. It is a community that is to be defined by his life, death, and resurrection.[1] And so those two Luke tagged as "men in white," they turned to the church staring up toward heaven and said, "This Jesus, who has been taken up from you into heaven, will come in the same way as you saw him go into heaven." Ascension II. The version that assumes a community of faith. It's not just about Ascension; it tells of the Lord's coming again. As in "he shall come to judge the quick and the dead."

My sermon preparation included two very disconcerting experiences this week. The first came as I decided to do a bit of online research into what has now become labeled as "rapture fiction." "Rapture" here refers to a particular end-time scenario espoused by fundamentalists or dispensationalists whereby

---

1. Beverly Gaventa, *Acts* in *Abingdon New Testament Commentaries* (Nashville: Abingdon Press, 2003), pp. 64-65.

Christians are spared from the great torment of the end of the world, the great battles, the wrath of God. This kind of fiction is typified by the best-selling "Left Behind" series, a current expression of what was represented thirty years ago by Hal Lindsey and his *Late Great Planet Earth.* My Web work this week led me to all sorts of places, to all sorts of titles, to all sorts of preachers, to all sorts of opinions that involve not just fiction and rapture and religion, but political movements and environmental policy and understandings of the Middle East and dangerous interpretations of current events. All of it, judging from just a bit of browsing, wildly popular. All of it, for me, hugely horrifying. I found myself agreeing with one author quoted in the *Christian Century,* who offered a critique of "rapture fiction" and its distorted theology. She suggested this summary paraphrase: "For God so loved the world, that God gave it World War III."

And this is my second disconcerting experience of the week. I rise to confess to you that in almost twenty years of weekly preaching, with a sermon number now rapidly reaching one thousand, in my nineteen years of parish ministry in the Presbyterian Church (USA), I have never really preached a sermon on the Second Coming of Christ. I have prayed about it, even in public: "Come, Lord Jesus!" I have preached on John 14:3: "If I go and prepare a place for you, I will come again and will take you to myself, so that where I am, there you may be also." In Advent I have preached on the difference between waiting for and preparing for Christ to come again. I know I have pointed out in sermons that the faithful are not intended to know the date and the time, that Christ shall come "like a thief in the night." Indeed, I have affirmed on more than one occasion that our future and the world's future still rest secure in the mercy and the plan of God. But what about Christ's Second Coming and what it will be like or how it will happen or what we are to believe?

I'm pretty sure I haven't really preached on "he shall come to judge the quick and the dead." And I'm pretty sure I'm not in the minority when it comes to mainline Protestant preachers like myself. So should we be surprised that so many, so many far from the fundamentalist pews, so many who would never turn to an electronic preacher or a Web site entitled "End Times," that still so many of us settle for an understanding of the Second Coming of Christ that comes from the best-seller shelf over there at Borders?

"This Jesus, who has been taken up from you into heaven, will come in the same way as you saw him go into heaven." This Jesus. Luke's same Jesus, going and coming. Luke's Jesus, who said, "Blessed are you who are poor, for yours is the kingdom of God. Blessed are you who are hungry now, for you will be filled. Blessed are all you who weep now, for you will laugh" (6:20-21). Luke's Jesus, who told the parables of the Good Samaritan, the Lost Coin, the Lost Sheep, and the Prodigal Son. Luke's Jesus, who healed the crippled woman on the Sabbath; who healed the ten lepers, including the nine who forgot to say thank you; who called Zacchaeus out of the tree and brought salvation to his house; who wept over Jerusalem, saying, "If you had only recognized the things that make for peace." Luke's Jesus, who joined those two disciples along the Emmaus Road. Their hearts burned within as he taught them from Scripture; their eyes were opened when he broke bread with them, and they recognized him.

This Jesus will come again in the same way as you saw him go up into heaven. This Jesus going and coming. The same way. The sameness Luke refers to — it has to be more than the mode of divine transportation. The emphasis is on this Jesus, the only Son of God, our Savior, who healed the sick, fed the hungry, rattled the powerful, and welcomed the sinner. He is the one who is coming. This Jesus. "From thence he shall come to judge the quick and the dead." Don't just stand there. Don't just stand there trying to figure out the calendar, or trying to predict the future, or trying to fathom the space involved in "From thence he shall come. . . ." From thence. From there. It's not about cosmology. It's about theology. It's about understanding this Jesus. As Daniel Migliore confidently proclaims, Christ comes from there, "from the omnipotent love of God . . . not from the anger and wrath of the God [of apocalyptic horrors] . . . not from the resources of the church, from the treasures of your personal religious experience, or from the vitalities and movements of history. . . . Christ will come from where only God can come . . . from the all-powerful and all-transforming love of God."[2] Or, in Luke's terms, this Jesus will come in the same way! This Jesus. You know him, and you know his Gospel.

He is coming again to judge the quick and the dead, which means everything, everyone, every time. The whole ball of wax. From soup to nuts. From A to Z. The whole world. Individuals. Institutions. Corporations. Nations. This whole blasted mess of a world we live in, including, of course, you and me. Christ shall judge. Judgment that is more than good from bad, more than sheep over here, goats over there, more than mighty wrath poured out like hot grease from a pan, more than just punishment, more than retribution. This judgment of the living and the dead, it seems to me, is intended to make all things right, to make all things new, to restore creation, to establish the kingdom, to bring about a new heaven and a new earth, to inaugurate and install a unique life lived forever in the light of God, for there will be no more night, and no more death, nor mourning, nor crying, nor pain, for the former things will be no more. God will wipe away every tear. And we shall see God's face. And God will be with us. God with us. Emmanuel. This Jesus. This same Jesus going and coming. He is coming to judge the living and the dead.

You probably won't find the Heidelberg Catechism on the shelf at Borders. The Heidelberg Catechism of 1562. If you find it, it won't be in the best-seller section. I'm sure you could find it on the Web. But when you are in doubt about the doctrines of faith,

2. Daniel Migliore, "From There He Will Come to Judge the Living and Dead: *Inde venturus est iudicare vivus et martuos*," in *Exploring and Proclaiming the Apostles' Creed*, edited by Roger E. Van Harn (Grand Rapids: William B. Eerdmans Publishing Company, 2004), p. 185.

when your preachers leave you frustrated for lack of attention, try plunging the depths of our own Presbyterian and Reformed tradition. Ponder point 52 in the Catechism:

Q. What comfort does the return of Christ "to judge the living and dead" give you?

A. That in all affliction and persecution I may await with head held high the very Judge from heaven. . . .

Christ Jesus is judge. You know him, and you know his gospel.

Centuries later, theologian Karl Barth summed it up this way: "To fear the last judgment is a pagan idea, not a Christian idea. There is only one who might be against us: Jesus Christ. And it is he, precisely, who is for us! . . . From Christmas on to the Return," Barth writes of this great truth, "I bring you good news of great joy!"[3] This same Jesus coming, going, and coming.

Robert Wuthnow co-edited a book entitled *The Quiet Hand of God: Faith-Based Activism and the Public Role of Mainline Protestantism.* In the introduction to the volume, the editors suggest that mainliners don't claim to be "exclusive mouthpieces of God," nor do they "selectively cite Bible verses to show why one manifestation of evil is so much worse than others." On the contrary, mainliners seek to discover and tap into "deeper truths about love, redemption, reconciliation, and justice," pervasive themes in the biblical tradition. "Understanding these truths and finding ways to put them into practice," Wuthnow concludes, "requires the church above all to function as a church — preaching and teaching, gathering for worship, praying and serving."[4]

3. Karl Barth, *The Faith of the Church: A Commentary on the Apostles' Creed according to Calvin's Catechism,* edited by Jean Louis Leuber, translated by Gabriel Vahanian (New York: Meridian Books, 1958), p. 118.

4. Robert Wuthnow, *The Quiet Hand of God: Faith-Based Activism and the Public Role of Mainline Protestantism* (Berkeley and Los Angeles: University of California Press, 2002), pp. 21-22.

Our response to the Second Coming is to be the church: to feed the hungry, to get the thirsty something to drink, to welcome the stranger, to clothe the naked, to take care of the sick, to visit those in prison. Maybe I was too hard on myself and my colleagues earlier. For the church has been talking about and living about and serving about the Second Coming. "From thence he shall come to judge the quick and the dead." You and I and the least of these. It's the same Jesus and his gospel.

"Why do you stand looking up toward heaven? This Jesus, who has been taken up from you into heaven, will come in the same way as you saw him go into heaven." Don't just stand there. Hold your head high. And go be the church!

Saved

MATTHEW 21:1-11

The Palm Sunday service was over. I was standing at the church door saying good-bye to the lingering few in every congregation who just don't want the fellowship to end. Palm Sunday was later that year, so spring was already in high gear. It was a beautiful day, and the sun was streaming into the narthex. The carpet in the narthex was strewn with little strips and threads of branches, the kind that wrap around the roller on the vacuum cleaner. A rather sorry lot of palm fronds still stood in the container that the ushers had used when handing them out. The wise ushers of that congregation used an old wrought-iron umbrella holder to organize, fan, and display the fronds. Now, seriously picked over, the few runt-like branches left looked more like an onion-grass bouquet picked by a three-year-old to be proudly given to his mother when an ordinary trip to the park suddenly became a memorable occasion. We were getting ready to close the door when a few strangers rushed up the steps. "Father, can we get some palm fronds?" one shouted. "I guess we have a few left," I said as I pointed to the multi-tasking umbrella holder. "Oh, thank goodness!" she said.

"We just have to get some every year." She grabbed several and handed them to her friends, and then they hustled down the steps and into the car that was waiting there in traffic. I don't even think they missed the green light. "We just have to get some every year."

In Matthew's Gospel, Palm Sunday begins as Jesus and the disciples draw near to Jerusalem. From the Mount of Olives, Jesus sends two of them ahead to obtain the royal means of transportation. Matthew is the only Gospel writer who mentions both a colt and a foal as he frames the Palm Sunday story in terms of the Old Testament reference as promise and fulfillment. Matthew hedges his interpretive bet on the prophet's Hebrew text: "Lo, your king comes to you; triumphant and victorious is he, humble and riding on a donkey, on a colt, the foal of a donkey" (Zech. 9:9). So the disciples do as they are told and bring both back for the inaugural parade. The reader is left to chuckle a bit at Matthew's preference for the two, trying to imagine how Jesus sat on both of them now that the disciples had put their cloaks on them.

As you realize with your listening ear that Matthew never identifies the spread branches as palm fronds, I invite you to hear as well Matthew's attention to the crowd. "A very large crowd spread their cloaks on the road." It was "the crowds that went ahead of Jesus and that followed." When Jesus arrived in Jerusalem, "the whole city was in turmoil, asking, 'Who is this?'" But it was the crowds who were saying, "This is the prophet Jesus from Nazareth in Galilee." When Luke tells the story, he references "the whole multitude of the disciples." When Mark tells the story, he comments on "those who went before and those who followed" in the procession. But Matthew — Matthew tells about the crowds.

Like the crowds that followed Jesus back in the early days "from Galilee, the Decapolis, Jerusalem, Judea, and from beyond the Jordan" (4:25). Like the crowds that he saw as he went up the mountain and sat down to offer the Beatitudes, those crowds who were "astounded at his teaching" when he finished that Sermon on the Mount (5:1; 7:28). Like the crowds that saw him heal the paralytic: "they were filled with awe, and they glorified God" (9:8). As Jesus became aware of the Pharisees' plans to destroy him, he departed. But "many crowds followed him, and he cured all of them" (12:15). When Jesus took the five loaves and two fish and blessed them and broke the loaves, it was the crowds who were sitting down on the grass, the crowds who were fed by the disciples (14:19). And of course, there at the trial before Pilate, the chief priests and elders "persuaded the crowds to ask for Barabbas and to have Jesus killed" (27:20). I'm not suggesting that the vocabulary of a crowd is theologically loaded for Matthew, that the word itself connotes something in particular. But I would suggest that here in Matthew, you can't look for the palm fronds. You have to look at the crowds!

"The crowds that went ahead of him and that followed were shouting." And they weren't shouting, "I believe in Jesus Christ, his only Son, our Lord, who was conceived by the Holy Ghost, born of the Virgin Mary, suffered under Pontius Pilate, was crucified, dead, and buried." They were shouting, "Save, save, save us!" "Hosanna to the Son of David! Blessed is the one who comes in the name of the Lord! Hosanna in the highest heaven!" "Hosanna," which means "O save!" The crowds. They weren't getting everything right. Jesus was more than a prophet from Nazareth in Galilee. But they were pleading to be saved. The crowds. No doubt some would soon be shouting for a crucifixion. But here they were shouting for salvation. Hosanna! Save! Save!

The crowds — they went ahead and they followed. They weren't just sitting there at the curb. There was movement. There was going ahead, and there was following. It was no lawn-chair crowd fit only for a turn of the head. The whole parade was headed for Jerusalem: Jesus, the donkey, the colt, the disciples, the crowds. All headed to the city of peace, where a pageant of salvation was to be played out through betrayal, suffering, death, and life. This was no "grab your palm and run" kind of crowd. Matthew

73

describes the crowd as moving along, which doesn't quite seem strong enough when you're talking about a procession that includes cross and resurrection. The crowd, they went ahead and they followed, begging to be saved. Shouting, that they might have a share in Jesus' life, death, and resurrection!

Like a Palm Sunday crowd that gathers at the font, standing elbow to elbow, arm in arm, with toes eagerly awaiting the next wave of God's grace. Here at this fount, our celebration is more than a sacramental washing, more than a ritualized welcome, more than a ceremonial invoking of the Holy Spirit. For here, when the crowd steps up and moves into the baptismal river, we know ourselves to be participating in Christ's death and resurrection. We are yearning to go before and to follow after down that Palm Sunday road. Or, to use the language of the Apostle Paul in the sixth chapter of his Letter to the Romans, "Do you not know that all of us who have been baptized into Christ Jesus were baptized into his death? Therefore we have been buried with him by baptism into death, so that, just as Christ was raised from the dead by the glory of the Father, so we too might walk in newness of life" (6:3-4).

This crowd, ahead and following, is traveling. This is not a crowd wandering along the road less traveled, demanding success or seeking the motivation of a purpose-driven life, expecting arrogant shouts of doctrinal correctness or role-modeled lives of self-proclaimed faith-filled perfection. No, this is a crowd whose identity and humility and hospitality and fragility come from Christ and Christ alone. This crowd movement along the path with Christ — it is toward his cross and resurrection. And we shall shout as we go. Save! Save! Save us!

It's a Palm Sunday procession that's going somewhere. In the power of the Holy Spirit, and by God's matchless grace, we are once again invited, called, drawn toward the very holiness of God revealed in the death and resurrection of Jesus Christ. That sacred space — it isn't found down the road; it doesn't just come later in the week. It occupies the very center of God's relationship with us and with all creation. The cross and the resurrection. The mystery of God's plan of salvation. God's love poured out. Christ emptying himself. God raising him on the third day. You and I, and the crowd, ahead and following, traveling to the holy of holies, to the heart of God, bound to Christ and his death and resurrection.

Which is all to say, I believe in the communion of saints. "I believe in the Holy Ghost, the holy catholic church, the communion of saints, the forgiveness of sins, the resurrection of the body, and the life everlasting." This is the part of the Creed where the conductor begs us to retard, and to enunciate, and to not take a breath because the Holy Spirit is in fact made known to us in the church, and among the saints, and in the forgiveness of sins.

The communion of saints. A simple affirmation of the fellowship of the church. We are one body. The communion of saints. A reference to our fellowship with those who have gone before, a mystical slice of the church visible and invisible, not just our fellowship with the martyrs and the bigwigs, but with Aunt Mame, and Grandma Rae, and Miss Thomas, and Mr. Ward. The communion of saints. A liturgical footnote that points to those who partake of holy things, as in the communion elements of bread and wine. A liturgical reference to the mystical union of communion fellowship, where Christ is one with us, and we are one with all who share the meal. The communion of saints. *Sanctorum Communio.*

A crowd of those who go ahead and those who follow, a crowd on the move, bound forever to the cross of Christ and his resurrection. A crowd of followers who know themselves to be drawn, to be called over and over again to the hill of Calvary and to the stone now rolled away. Or, as one theologian puts it, "a community of those who, being united with Jesus, wait for the future of God, and live their lives with such expectation."[1] The com-

1. Wolfhart Pannenberg, *The Apostles' Creed in the Light of Today's Questions,* translated by Margaret Kohl (Philadelphia: Westminster Press, 1972), p. 154.

munion of saints. A procession of those who partake of the holiest of things, those whose identity and humility and hospitality and fragility come from Christ and Christ alone. A crowd full of those who find themselves once again with Christ, heading toward his cross and resurrection. And shouting as we go. Save! Save! Save us!

"Father, can we get some palm fronds?" I guess if I'm honest and a bit of a realist, I see that woman all the time. Indeed, the church is called to a life of servanthood, certainly serving those who are looking to grab a palm frond and go. Every congregation includes those who partake of the community's life from the fringe — commitment on their own terms; a consumer approach to picking and choosing programs; some idea that what goes on here is good for children only; an a la carte approach that allows for music only, or education only, or mission only, or youth activities only; an understanding of finance and stewardship that somehow concludes that if you give only to what you like, someone else will pay the heating and lighting bills and the salaries; an experience of worship that views the preacher of the day as a reason to choose whether or not to come to church on Sunday. The church is full of folks who would prefer to grab a palm and go, all the while patting themselves on the back: "At least we're not like those Christmas and Easter folks."

The problem is this: the gift, the promise, the invitation is that God is calling us to the communion of saints.

Behold!

1 CORINTHIANS 15:50-58; MATTHEW 28:1-10

⌒ᴍᴄ⌒

"I believe in the resurrection of the body and the life everlasting" — these are the last two affirmations of the Apostles' Creed. After five weeks of Lent and one Palm Sunday, we have come to the end of this creedal preaching series. The resurrection of the body and the life everlasting. Our Easter Day proclamation. One of my children, like other growing children who find it harder and harder to attribute any wisdom at all to their parents, was quite amused by the coincidence: that we would arrive at "the resurrection of the body" on Easter Sunday! For our visitors this morning, let me say that we've been working pretty hard in our preaching life these last six weeks. And so today we stand outside the empty tomb with shouts of acclamation. "Christ is risen! He is risen indeed!" But here at the empty tomb, we also find ourselves dangling at the end of the Apostles' Creed, just before the period, trying to grapple with "I believe in the resurrection of the body and the life everlasting." And so the preacher Paul rises among us, the Apostle Paul and his First Epistle to the Corinthians. In his best Easter voice, Paul shouts above all the commotion and the celebration, "Behold, behold! I will tell you a mystery!" (KJV; NSRV).

It's one of the most common questions a pastor is asked when teaching a class on the Creed or leading a discussion with people exploring membership in the church, the question about "the resurrection of the body." Folks often ask about "he descended into hell," or they want to make sure that in the phrase "holy catholic church" the word "catholic" means "universal," as in the broad witness of the Christian church. But experience tells me that questions about "the resurrection of the body" are soon to follow. Will we recognize each other? What about this body? Will we have wings? Earth burial or cremation — does it matter in the resurrection? Does it happen immediately, as with Jesus' words to the thief on the cross ("Today you will be with me in paradise"), or does it happen later, not until the last trumpet, more along Paul's time line in First Corinthians? Resurrection of the body — yeah, how's that going to happen?

I've come to the conclusion that my pastoral answers haven't always been the most theologically thorough. My first response to "resurrection of the body" questions has usually been to cite the bodily resurrection of Jesus of Nazareth. You remember those Easter stories of the risen Christ told by Luke and John. Resurrection accounts that go beyond empty tombs and grave clothes left in a laundry pile, accounts that include voices and conversation and a desire to embrace, accounts that tell of scarred hands, feet, and side, stories that include bread broken, meals shared, fishermen stripped for work, breakfast fixed there on the beach. The bodily resurrection of Jesus of Nazareth, the one who was crucified, dead, and buried. God raised him from the dead. There was no life in him, but in the power of God, death could not hold him.

The bodily resurrection of Jesus affirms the totality of God's victory over death and puts an exclamation point on God's transcendence as, with a certain earthiness, the risen Christ baptizes this world with his presence and commissions the church to be his body in service to this world. And these Gospel narratives that tell of hands and feet and side — they haunt those who would prefer a safer, more acceptable, more spiritual encounter that separates body from soul and allows some part of existence to live on with singing birds, and flowing streams, and a great circle of life. This "Jesus who was crucified. He is not here; for he has been raised, as he said. Come, see the place where he lay." That's what the angel said on Easter morning. It's the resurrection of his body.

"Behold! I will tell you a mystery!" Paul's Easter voice again. "Behold, I will tell you a mystery! We will not all die, but we will all be changed, in a moment, in the twinkling of an eye, at the last trumpet. For the trumpet will sound, and the dead will be raised imperishable, and we will be changed. For this perishable body must put on imperishability. . . ." "Pastor, it's not just about his body." That would seem to be Paul's response to my frail efforts to teach a theology of resurrection. This mystery. It's not just about his body, it's about ours: our flesh, our bones, our lives, our humanity, our world. "I believe in the resurrection of the body and the life everlasting." The resurrection of the flesh. The resurrection of human flesh.

When I have the opportunity to teach preaching at the seminary down the block, the students in the Introduction to Preaching class are usually assigned a funeral homily to write and to deliver. It is a very practical and helpful assignment. Every year a conversation plays out in the class in some shape or form. It involves the question of delivering a sermon in witness to the resurrection when officiating at a funeral for someone the pastor doesn't know. More to the point, what if the pastor doesn't know anything about the deceased person's faith — or lack thereof? Students agonize about what to say, how to approach the task, how to choose words carefully, how to maintain a certain theological integrity, as if the primary theological task of preaching at a funeral is to declare whether someone "made it" or didn't, got into heaven or didn't. The preacher as sports broadcaster. "Goal! Goal! Goal!"

A service in witness to the resurrection is no more dependent upon an individual's faith than our celebration of Easter is dependent upon our ability to figure it all out or to work out the time line or to know which one of our earthly bodies will get the best eternal makeover. For when the followers of Jesus are confronted by everything that death has to offer, the church as preacher rises to proclaim the power of God to bring life out of death, the power of God to transform the dark shadows of despair into the rising light of a bright morning star, the power of God to anoint the sufferings of this life with a hope-filled balm of the kingdom yet to come. "Preacher, it's not about this body, or that body, or that body." The resurrection of the body and the life everlasting. It is about God's resurrection power: the perishable putting on imperishability, the mortal putting on immortality. It's not just the Apostle Paul and his Easter voice now. It is all of creation standing to sing and to stomp. "Death has been swallowed up in victory. Where, O death, is your victory? Where, O death, is your sting?"

When the end of the Apostles' Creed coincidentally meets the dawn of Easter Day, a sentimental nod to resurrection won't do. Nor, frankly, can we settle for a rather privatized assurance of or self-centered concern for "me and my body" at the heavenly gates, as in "I believe in the resurrection of my body"! No, for Matthew would have you know that this is a resurrection of seismic proportions. When Mary Magdalene and the other Mary went to see the tomb, Matthew reports a great earthquake, and an angel of the Lord descending from heaven, and a rolling back of that stone that served as death's door, and an angel with a bit of an attitude sitting on that boulder. The very messenger of God reclining on death's door as the whole world recovers from its shaking. Don't miss that message here. Some would point out the cosmic symbolism. Theologians would point to the apocalyptic imagery of earthquakes and angels. One preacher points out that the call to worship that first Easter morning was far from a cheery "Good morning."[1] That shattering earthquake. A stone rolled away. An angel reclining on death's door. God taking on the powers of sin and death and chaos and evil and suffering, and the angel sitting on that stone. I think it's God talking smack. A bit of divine trash talk. Resurrection on the first Easter morning. Resurrection with an attitude!

Because resurrection of the body — it's not just his body. It's not just my body or yours. Resurrection of the body is all about God's eternal embrace of the dry bones of our humanity. God's everlasting hope for creation, for the world God has made. Easter morning. Resurrection day. It's all about God's confrontation with a world of death. A world so wedded to violence and war. A world sold on the power of sin. As one preacher put it, "Easter is not a morning for artful arguments, subtle distinctions, the stuff of academic seminars." Easter is "confrontation of the highest order,"[2] not just a song but a stomp! This resurrection victory of life over death. That you and I might comprehend our whole life, this life and the next, in the splendor of Christ's mercy, of his grace, and of his power. That we might comprehend not simply God's love for us, but God's love for the world.

Resurrection of the body. When the perishable puts on imperishability, and the mortal puts on immortality, then shall come to pass a kingdom. Not just pearly gates and roads paved with gold, not just a heavenly city far from our imagination, but a kingdom of God that you and I can imagine, a kingdom we can taste, a kingdom we glimpse, where high schools are no longer killing fields, and there is no such thing as a second anniversary of a war that's still going on, and one woman's suffering need not be used for political gain, and a term like "cancer" will just be a word to be spat upon, and children will not be left parentless, and hard-

1. Thomas G. Long, *Matthew* (Louisville: Westminster/John Knox, 1997), p. 323.

2. Peter J. Gomes, *Sermons: Biblical Wisdom for Daily Living* (New York: William Morrow & Co., 1998), pp. 73-74.

working families will not be labeled as unwanted immigrants and treated as worse. The resurrection of the body and the life everlasting. God's eternal embrace of the dry bones of our humanity. God's piercing light that illumines all that life is to be.

"Behold! I will tell you a mystery!" The Apostle Paul in his Easter voice. "Therefore, my beloved," says Paul, the Easter-morning preacher, and he turns and points to the church and to the world, and when he points, you see that the sleeves are already rolled up, ready to get to work. He turns and points to us today.

"Therefore, my beloved, be steadfast, immovable, always excelling in the work of the Lord."

Easter people with an attitude.